D0991522

Brian Wildsmith's

ILLUSTRATED BIBLE STORIES

Brian Wildsmith's ILLUSTRATED BIBLE STORIES

As told by

PHILIP TURNER

FRANKLIN WATTS, INC.

575 LEXINGTON AVENUE NEW YORK N.Y. 10022

First published 1968 by Oxford University Press
First American publication 1969 by Franklin Watts, Inc.
Library of Congress Catalog Card Number: 68-14250
Printed in Austria

CONTENTS

THE OLD TESTAMENT

God Made Everything

Before the beginning there was only God and nothing else at all. On the first day that all things started, God sent His Spirit winging over the emptiness that was not Himself, like a white bird over a grey and tumbling sea.

On the first day God said, "Let there be light," and the sun came up like a shining new penny over the empty sea, and that first night there was a riding moon, and the stars were like a million holes in a blue velvet sky.

Then there was a week of making, such a week as God had not known before. Dry land came like a whale out of the water, and on the land, grass—green as gooseberries—and gooseberries themselves, and great trees thrusting up out of the warm earth, their leaves whispering in astonishment at the breeze. In the sea below the untrodden beach there was the silver flicker of a thousand kinds of fish, and beneath them in the great deeps the sea monsters, Leviathan and his kind.

To fly in the sky, God made winged creatures: butterflies, pretty as paint; dragon-flies like jewels in the air; and all manner of birds—from the one-inch humming-bird which can also fly backwards, to the great albatross soaring over the ocean like the Spirit of God Himself.

God made creatures to live on the dry land. He made the dappled fawn standing in the glade by the pool. He made the giraffe, so proud, so very proud, saying to all beneath him, "Oh, who but me has a neck like a fire-escape?"

3

He made the lynx with the long tail, and the manx cat with no tail, and the wise grey elephant with legs like logs and a tail at both ends. From the small snail with his fragile house on his back to the tawny lion, king of the jungle and needing no house, God made them all.

Last of all, God said, "I will make man. I will make him in my likeness and after my image." So out of the dust of the earth God formed the first man and breathed life into his nostrils. And the first man, Adam, stood on the new earth and looked into the eyes of God. And he was not afraid.

The Garden of Eden

God made a garden for Adam to live in. It was called Eden, and it was very beautiful. Adam was happy caring for the garden and ruling the animals and walking with God in the cool of the evening when the day's work was done.

There came an evening when Adam was unusually silent as they walked. God looked at the man. "Tell me your sorrow, Adam," He said. "Lord," replied Adam, "what is sorrow? Yet there is something in my heart. See the animals," and he pointed to where the lion lay crouched for the night beside his mate.

"The lion has the lioness, the stag has the doe for company. Of every creature you have made two—except of me."

"Your feeling is called 'loneliness'," said God. "It is not good that you should be alone."

He caused a deep sleep to fall on Adam. And there in the dusk, while the garden and all the animals slept, He called forth a mate for Adam, making her mysteriously out of the very bone of Adam's body.

Adam awoke and found her beside him; Eve, the first woman. She was like him, and yet she was wonderfully and mysteriously different, as the mountain pool is like, yet different from the waterfall that fills it.

6

The Coming of Sorrow

Adam and Eve were happy in the garden where God had made them lord and lady of everything. Only one thing was forbidden them. In the heart of the garden there grew a tree, the Tree of the Knowledge of Good and Evil. "You may eat the fruit of all the trees in the garden," said God, "except that one. If you do you will surely die."

"What is 'die'?" Eve asked Adam when they were snug in their bower for the night. But Adam did not know. "What is Evil?" asked Eve. But Adam did not know that either.

There came a day when Adam was busy, and Eve strayed by the Tree of the Knowledge of Good and Evil. She gazed at it, wondering.

"Eat," said a voice. Eve spun round and there, gazing at her with eyes like rubies, was a serpent greener than the grass.

"Eat and be wise," said the serpent.

"We may not," said Eve, her hands to her mouth. "For if we do we shall die."

"You will not die," said the serpent, "you will become wise. You will be as God Himself, knowing Good and Evil."

So in a sad hour Eve plucked fruit from the tree and ate. And as she did so a

7

cold wind shivered over the garden as if all nature mourned. When Adam discovered what Eve had done he was heartbroken. But out of his love for her, and so that he might share her dying, he too took and ate the dark fruit.

That evening God came and called as at other times: "Adam! Adam!" But Adam did not come. He huddled with Eve in the dark depths of a thicket for they were ashamed and frightened. When God found them He did not need to ask what they had done. It was all too plain in their faces. With infinite sadness He told them what now must surely follow. Nature would grow wild, the earth blighted, the animals savage. They must leave the garden and make their lonely way in a hostile world until they grew old and died.

But God also made a promise. He made it a little sadly, knowing even then what it would one day cost.

"Eve," He said, "as the serpent has this day wounded your heel, so one day a child of yours shall crush his head."

So Adam, with his arm round the shoulder of Eve his wife, went out from Eden. Behind them, guarding the gate back to the garden of innocence, God set an angel with a flaming sword.

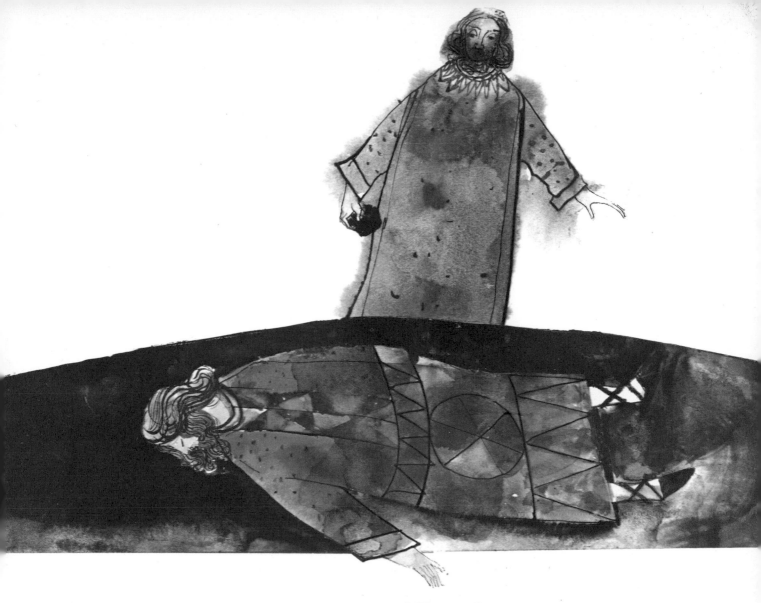

The Coming of Death

The first two of Eve's children were boys, Cain and Abel. Abel grew up to be a shepherd, but Cain was a gardener, and often they argued fiercely as to whether it was better to tend sheep or growing things.

One day Cain and Abel went out into the field to offer sacrifice to God. They laid their offerings on the altar and set fire to the wood. Abel's fire burned fierce and sweet, and the smoke went up to heaven like chimney smoke in a still dawn. But Cain's sacrifice would not burn, and the smoke hugged the ground like a bonfire in a wet autumn.

"God accepts my offering," shouted Abel in triumph. "Shepherds are better than gardeners."

Cain was furiously angry. He seized a stone and with one terrible blow felled his brother. When he saw what he had done he ran in terror and hid from God as his father had done before him.

9

But into his hiding-place as a sad cry on the wind came the voice of God: "Cain, Cain, where is your brother Abel?"

"Am I my brother's keeper?" Cain snarled at the empty sky.

Because of what he had done God condemned Cain to go from his parents and wander the earth. And God marked him with the sign of Cain so that all might know him and none should slay him. For a man is his brother's keeper, and one day God planned to show this truth to all mankind.

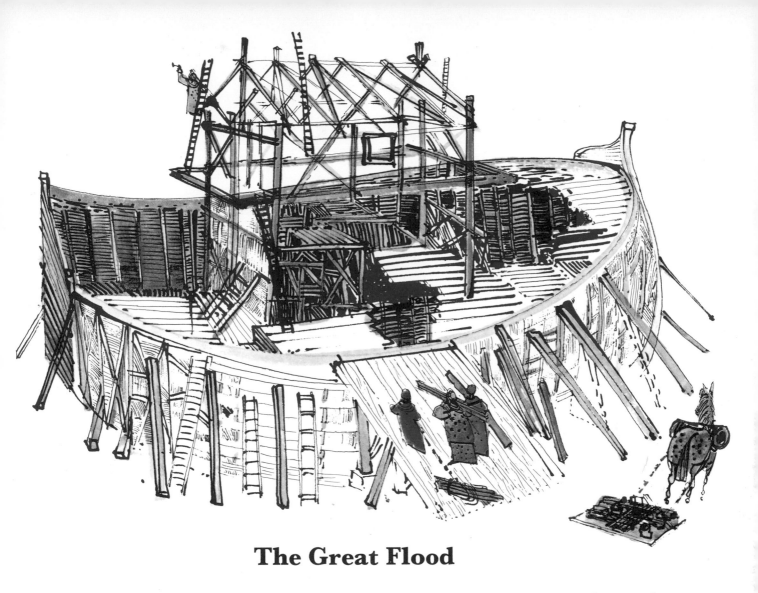

The Great Flood

Adam died and Eve died, and Cain, and Abel. Their children spread over the face of the earth and grew ever more wicked.

God looked out from heaven, and in the whole world He saw only one good man, Noah. All the rest was darkness and evil and violence.

"I will make an end," God cried. "I repent that I created man. I will destroy the earth I have made. Only Noah shall be saved."

God caused Noah to make a great ship, an ark. Vast, it towered like a cliff over Noah's house. When the ark was ready God called all the animals. Two lions from the jungle, two giraffes from the plains, two camels from the desert; two of every kind, they came stamping and snorting and roaring and whinnying into the ark. Noah and his family followed and drew up the gang-plank.

All was ready.

Then it rained. It rained and it rained and it rained. It rained until the puddles became floods and the floods became lakes and the lakes joined up with the seas, and Noah could not distinguish the water pouring on to the deck from the water lapping under the hull of the ark.

Then it stopped.

Noah opened a window and looked out. All the earth to the top of the highest mountain was covered with water, and every living thing was drowned.

The sun shone, the wind blew, and the water started to go down. Down it went, and down and down, until one day Noah sent out a raven to look for land. But the raven could find nowhere to perch, so in the evening it came winging back to the ark.

The sun shone, the wind blew, and the water went down. Now Noah sent out a tiny white dove. Around she flew, and around, then she flew out of sight. That evening she came back. In her beak she carried a twig of green olive. Noah gazed at it in great wonder, tears in his eyes, so delicate it seemed, the first growing thing since the great flood.

At last the ark grounded on the slopes of Mount Ararat. Noah threw down the gang-plank and stepped ashore on to the blessed earth, he and his family, the only human beings in a world swept clean. Stamping and snorting and roaring and whinnying, the animals—now many more than two of each kind— came thundering after them. They leapt and rolled for joy on the brave new grass, and forgetting all about Noah who had saved them, they ran away into the forest. As Noah gazed after them, there appeared over the mountain in a great round arch, a shining bow of many colours, the first rainbow. And the voice of God spoke from beyond the rainbow as Noah kneeled on the earth:

"I set my bow in the heavens as a sign and a promise. While the earth remains I will never again smite every living thing. For the heart of man is twisted and he cannot, without my help, walk in my ways."

And that very night, as if to prove the truth of what God had said, old Noah got so terribly drunk with wine that his sons had to put him to bed. And he was the one good man who had been saved from the flood.

Abraham and Isaac

Many years later, when the earth was once again peopled, there lived in the city of Ur a shepherd called Abraham.

One day as he was tending his flocks, he heard a voice calling on the wind.

"Abraham," said the voice. "Leave your country and your father's house. I will lead you to a land I have chosen for you. I will bless you and make your name great. And in your children shall all the families of the earth be blessed."

"It is the Lord," said Abraham. "I will obey."

For many years he wandered with his wife Sarah, his household and his flocks, until he came to the borders of the land of Canaan.

As he gazed down on that lovely land and thought how wonderful it would be to end his weary wanderings and settle in those green pastures, God spoke to him again.

"Abraham, I will give this land to your children."

That was all. But before he moved on, Abraham built an altar, and burned a sacrifice to show that he had heard the voice, even though he did not understand how the words could ever come true since he and his wife were old and they had no children.

In God's good time there came a day, a great day in Abraham's life, when he and his wife were visited by an angel of God. The angel prophesied that in due time Sarah would bear a son. So it turned out. And they called the child Isaac.

Isaac grew to be a fine boy, and Abraham never tired of watching him and pondering how good God had been to him. But one day as he pondered, it seemed to him that God again spoke to him.

"Abraham," the voice said, "do you love me?"

"Yes," he replied.

"Then take what you love most of all and sacrifice it to me."

Abraham paused long before he replied, for it was Isaac that he loved most.

"It is the Lord," he said. "I will do even as he says."

He took wood for the sacrifice, and the sacrificial knife, and he saddled his donkey and led his son to the place of sacrifice high in the mountains. He built an altar, he laid the wood in place, and then he stretched Isaac upon it.

He took the terrible sacrificial knife and held it high over his head. And even as he did so, he heard the voice of God calling, calling from heaven.

"Now I know that you love me," cried the voice, "since you have not withheld even your beloved son. I will bless you and multiply your children as the stars of the night sky and the sand on the seashore. And in your children shall all the nations of the earth be blessed." The voice ceased and there was only the wind on the bare mountain.

With a singing heart Abraham released his son, and in Isaac's place they offered to God a ram caught by his horns in a thicket. And so they came down from the mountain.

Jacob

Isaac, when he became a man, married a woman called Rebecca, and they had two children, twins called Jacob and Esau.

The two boys were very different. Esau was a rugged, hairy man, a fine hunter, and his father's favourite. But Rebecca loved best stay-at-home Jacob with his skin smooth as a woman's.

One day, when Isaac was an old man, he sent Esau out to hunt the fallow deer. "I am old," he said, "and blind. Make a dish of the venison that I love, and I will bless you before I die."

Now Rebecca had heard what Isaac had said, and she greatly desired to win his blessing for her own favourite, Jacob. As soon as Esau had gone out she made a dish of goat's meat, disguising it to seem like venison.

She took the hide of a goat and put it on the backs of Jacob's hands and his neck, so that they were rough like his brother's. Then she sent the boy to his father with the dish of meat.

"Venison such as you love," said Jacob.

"You have been quick, my son," the old man replied.

"The Lord God brought the deer to my bow," Jacob replied smoothly. But Isaac was suspicious. He made Jacob come close so that he could feel his hands.

"The voice is Jacob's," he said to himself, "but the hands are indeed those of Esau." So at last he was convinced. He ate the meal and then made Jacob kneel before him. He laid his hands on his son's head and blessed him, making him Lord and inheritor of all.

When Esau returned, his anger was so terrible that Jacob had to fly for his life, and Rebecca sent him to Haran to live with her brother. The journey was long and on the way Jacob had to camp in the open.

One night as he lay under the stars he dreamed. In his dream he saw a great ladder stretching up from the earth beyond the stars to the very gates of heaven. Up and down the ladder the messengers of God, the bright angels, journeyed at the Lord's bidding. From heaven God called to him in a great voice. A voice which his father would have recognized—and Abraham, and Noah, and Cain, and Adam.

"I am the Lord God of Abraham," cried the voice. "The land you lie on, I will give it to you and your children. And in your children shall all the families of the earth be blessed."

In the morning Jacob built an altar of stones to mark the place, and so went on his way.

Joseph

Jacob had twelve sons, and among them Joseph, next to youngest, was his favourite. Joseph's older brothers were jealous of him, especially when their father had a special gift woven for his favourite, a coat with all the colours of the rainbow.

But their jealousy turned to hatred because of two dreams which came to Joseph from God. He dreamed that all the family were in the fields binding sheaves of corn, and all the sheaves of all the family bowed down and did homage to his sheaf. And again he dreamed that he was a bright star in the sky, and the sun and moon and the other stars did him homage as a king.

So the brothers resolved to kill Joseph.

They were away from home tending the sheep when Joseph came to them, sent by their father. They seized the lad, and despite his cries, threw him into a deep sheer-sided pit and left him there to die. They took his many-coloured coat, dipped it into the blood of a goat and carried it home to Jacob.

"It is my son's coat," the old man said sadly. "Doubtless he has been killed by wild beasts. I will go down into the grave mourning for my son."

But Midianite merchants, slave-traders, came journeying by the pit where Joseph lay. They found him and pulled him out. They bound his hands and led him down into Egypt where they sold him as a slave to Potiphar, captain of the guard to great king Pharaoh himself.

20

Joseph rose high in Potiphar's household, but the captain's wife fell in love with him. When Joseph refused to return her love, it quickly turned to hatred, and she falsely accused him to her husband, who had him thrown into prison.

Among the captives were two others who had also fallen from high office, Pharaoh's butler and his baker.

One night the butler and the baker both dreamed. In the morning they told their dreams to Joseph.

"In my dream," said the butler, "there was a vine with three branches. They budded and blossomed and the grapes grew. I pressed the grapes into Pharaoh's cup, and behold, it became wine which I gave to my lord."

And God revealed to Joseph the meaning of the dream.

"The three branches are three days," he said. "In three days you will be restored to your high office and will carry wine to Pharaoh as in former days. And when you stand again before Pharaoh, remember me in this dark dungeon."

Then the baker told his dream.

"I had on my head three white baskets," he said, "full of bakemeats which I was carrying to Pharaoh. But the birds flew down out of the sky and ate up the bakemeats."

And again God revealed the dream to Joseph.

"The three baskets are three days," he said sadly. "In three days Pharaoh will take you from this prison and hang you, and the birds will eat the flesh from your bones."

And so it came about. The baker was executed, and the butler was restored to his high office. But when he walked again in the sunlit courts of his lord, the butler forgot Joseph and the promise he had made in the dark dungeon.

Two years passed. And then one night Pharaoh dreamed.

In his dream he stood by the great River Nile. Out of the river came seven fat cattle, followed by seven cattle so thin that they were like skeletons in leather bags. The thin cattle ate up the fat cattle, and then Pharaoh awoke. He rolled over in his golden bed and dreamed again. There were seven full, ripe ears of corn. And then there were seven thin ears, meagre as if they had been blasted by the east wind. As before, the thin ears consumed the full ears, and Pharaoh awoke. He called in haste for his wise men and his magicians, but none of them could tell what the dreams meant. Then the butler remembered Joseph and how he had interpreted the dreams in the dungeon. So Joseph was brought, blinking in the bright sun, to stand before Pharaoh.

22

"My God will tell you the meaning of the dream," he said. "The cattle and the ears of corn are years. There will be seven years of plenty followed by seven years of famine such as the world has never known. In the years of plenty Pharaoh must build granaries and store-houses, and pile up food against the years of famine."

So Pharaoh did as Joseph said, and he put Joseph himself in charge of the work. So Joseph rose high in the land of Egypt and was second only to great Pharaoh himself.

The seven years of plenty came and went, and then the famine struck. All the world was hungry, and people came from every land to buy food in Egypt. Among them came Joseph's brothers, sent by Jacob.

Joseph recognized them, but did not make himself known although his heart cried out to see Benjamin, his youngest brother, who had stayed at home with Jacob.

He sent his brothers home with corn in their sacks, telling them to come again with Benjamin, and keeping Simeon as hostage against their return. At last they came again to buy corn, and this time they brought Benjamin with them. Joseph was so moved that he could no longer carry on the deception. He made himself known and sent his brothers home again to tell Jacob that he was still alive.

The old man listened in silence to the strange tale. Then he raised his eyes to heaven.

"It is enough," he said. "Joseph my son is yet alive. I will go and see him before I die."

So Jacob packed all his family, his servants and his goods into the wagons Joseph had sent, and driving their flocks before them, they went down into Egypt. There they lived under Joseph's protection, and there in Egypt Jacob died. But because he had wished it, remembering the promises of God, they did not bury him in Egypt, but carried his body and laid it to rest beyond Jordan in the promised land of Canaan.

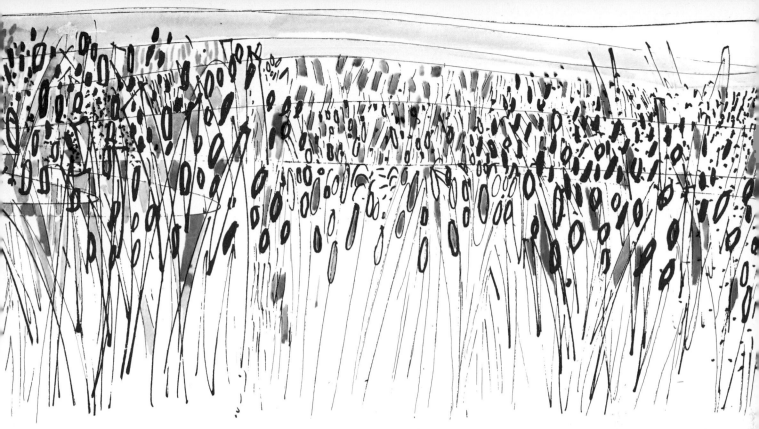

How Moses was Saved

Joseph died, and his master, and there arose a new Pharaoh who feared and hated the Children of Israel, as they were now called. He made their life miserable with harsh labour in the brickyards, and he passed terrible laws to keep them in slavery.

The worst of all these laws was one which said that of all children born to the Israelites, only the girls were to be allowed to live. The boys must be killed as soon as they were born.

One couple who could not bear to part with their baby boy, hid him away until he was three months old. At last, as his voice grew stronger, the mother knew that she must part with her baby. She made a little ark, like a cradle, out of rushes. She covered it with pitch to make it watertight. She put her sleeping son into the ark, and gently launched it on to the waters of the Nile. She watched it as it drifted slowly away, rocking gently, round the bend of the river and out of sight. Sadly, she went home.

Farther down the river Pharaoh's daughter was bathing with her maidens. She saw the ark and looked inside.

"It is one of the Israelite children," she cried. "What a beautiful little boy." She carried the baby home to her great palace and fed him and brought him up herself.

He was called Moses, which is Hebrew for "brought out", because, as Pharaoh's daughter said, "We brought him out of the water."

Moses Flies from Egypt

Moses grew up as an Egyptian prince, but because his parents were Israelites, he often went down to the crowded mud huts of Goshen, the slave quarter, where his own people lived.

One day in Goshen he came upon an Egyptian beating an Israelite slave. He ran to stop this cruelty, was soon involved in a fight, and a moment later the Egyptian lay dead at his feet.

Moses was very frightened, but he resolved to keep the matter secret. Helped by the Israelite he buried the dead man in the sand and went back to the palace.

When next he ventured into Goshen he came upon two Israelites fighting. He tried to part them and one of them turned on him in fury.

"Will you kill us as you killed the Egyptian?" he shouted.

Terrified that the thing was known, Moses returned to the palace in haste. In haste he saddled his horse, and carrying only a few necessities he fled from Egypt to hide himself in the desert.

28

God Calls Moses

In the wilderness Moses found work as a shepherd. One day, as he was tending his sheep on the slopes of Mount Horeb, he saw a strange sight: a bush which seemed to be ablaze with fire. Yet there was no smoke, and the bush was not destroyed.

Out of the burning bush a voice spoke: "I am the God of your fathers. The God of Abraham, of Isaac, and of Jacob." Moses bowed his head for he was afraid. "I have seen the sufferings of my people in Egypt," said the voice, "and I have come down to deliver them. To bring them to a good land, a land flowing with milk and honey, the land of Canaan. Moses, my servant, I send you to Pharaoh that you may lead my people out of Egypt."

Moses bowed until his face touched the ground.

"Who am I," he cried, "that I should appear before Pharaoh?"

"I am God," said the voice, "and I have sent you. Now go. And certainly I will be with you."

The voice ceased and there was only the wind on the mountain, and the bush was only a bush with Moses kneeling before it.

29

Out of Egypt

"The Lord, the God of Israel, says—'Let my people go.'" So spoke Moses before great Pharaoh in the sunlit presence-chamber in the palace by the Nile. But Pharaoh smiled a tight-lipped smile. "Who is the God of Israel that I should let this people go?" he said. "Lay more burdens upon them. They make bricks for my kingdom. Henceforth let them make them without straw."

Next day Moses met Pharaoh as he went to the sacred river to perform the office of a king.

"Thus says the Lord God of Israel," cried Moses: " 'The river shall be turned to blood, and the pools and the streams and the ponds. The fish shall die and the land shall stink.' "

And so it was. And after the blood there was a plague of frogs, so that men gathered them in heaps and the land stank again. And after the frogs a plague of lice, and then flies like a black sandstorm. There was a disease of the cattle. The people were afflicted with boils. There was thunder and hail, and in the storm Pharaoh sent for Moses. With the lightning flickering across the darkened windows of the presence-chamber, Pharaoh said, "I have sinned. The Lord is righteous, and my land is destroyed."

Moses replied, "As soon as the Children of Israel are gone from the city I will lift up my hands to the heavens and the storm shall cease."

"Go," said Pharaoh. But again he changed his mind, and when the storm ceased he would not let them leave the land.

Then came the locusts, a great black cloud of them darkening the heavens, and they ate up all green things in the land of Egypt. After the locusts, came a darkness so thick that it was like black velvet that you could touch in front of your eyes.

In the darkness, by the gleaming light of a lamp, one last time Moses and Pharaoh faced each other.

"Let my people go!" cried Moses.

"No! No! No!" shouted Pharaoh. "Take heed to yourself, adopted son of my daughter. Come to me no more. In the day that you see my face again, in that day you shall surely die."

With matching anger Moses replied, "You have spoken well, great Pharaoh. You shall see my face no more, and there shall indeed be death." He swept out into the darkness.

That night, at midnight, a great wailing cry arose across the sleeping city. For the dark angel of death struck with the last and most terrible of all the plagues—death for the firstborn. All died. From the heir of Pharaoh sitting upon his golden throne to the firstborn captive in the very dungeon, to all death came with the stroke of midnight.

In the night, even as death stalked in Egypt, the Israelites fled from their slave encampment. So that when a wan sun rose over the stricken land, Goshen was a ghost city of empty mud huts with the open doors creaking in the dawn breeze.

Over the Red Sea

In the dawning, as Pharaoh mourned over his stricken land, they told him that the Children of Israel had fled. His anger was terrible, and he sent his army in hot pursuit in chariots, on swift horses, with the foot-soldiers bringing up the rear.

Moses marched at the front of the long column of Israel, spread like a serpent over the shifting sand. Swift messengers came flying from the rear to tell him of the Egyptian pursuit. He stood on a rock and gazed back to the cloud of dust already darkening the horizon. He turned and gazed eastward to where the calm waters of the Red Sea lay, a shining barrier separating them from the safety of the true desert beyond.

"Do not be afraid," he cried to the upturned faces. "See the salvation of the Lord. After this day you shall see the Egyptians no more—for ever." He stretched out his staff, pointed it over the still water, and a great hush fell on all Israel.

With a shiver and a wrinkle on the water where Moses' staff pointed, a breeze began to blow. After the breeze came a strong wind roaring out of the east,

34

whipping Moses' hair before it like banners, and blowing back the shining water, piling it up until it was like a great wall, the yellow sand uncovered at its foot.

"Forward!" shouted Moses against the roaring of the wind, and the whole long column plunged across the uncovered sea-bed to the far shore and the start of the true desert.

Even as the tail of the serpent struggled on to the land, so the first chariots of Egypt skimmed down the beach and with never a pause rolled on across the sea-bed.

Moses waited until the whole pursuit was stretched out on the sand below them. Again he raised his staff and pointed. The roaring wind faltered and dropped to a breeze, to the flutter of a scarf, to a dead calm. The Red Sea came roaring back, terrible as thunder, a great white-capped tide faster than chariots, faster than horses.

In the morning the flower of the Egyptian army, men and horses, broken chariots and equipment was washed up like tide wrack along the shore of the Red Sea.

The Birth of a Nation

For forty years the Children of Israel wandered in the desert hardly knowing where they went, yet always haunted by the old promises of a golden land and of some great purpose in the world. Through the years the rabble of fearful slaves became an army of hardened warriors, for the desert was a stern land, killing all but the bold and strong.

At last they came to the mountain of Sinai, and Moses, who was now an old man, knew that here they would at last meet the God who had led them out of Egypt.

He left the people encamped round the foot of the mountain and alone set out to climb into the cloud and the flickering lightning which surrounded the summit. All Israel watched him go, a lone figure—so small—on the bare slopes of the mountain.

When Moses came back out of the cloud he was carrying two great tablets of stone with the law to govern Israel's future engraved upon them. As he came down the mountain his face shone with a light not of this world, for he had met God and talked with Him face to face.

That night, as they sat at peace and in safety round the bright camp-fires, Moses read to them what was written on the stones.

"Thou shalt have no other God but me."

"Thou shalt not take my name in vain."

"Keep holy the Sabbath day."

And the people murmured their assent. Each man gazed at his neighbour, red in the fire-light; saw his neighbour as his brother; knew deep in his heart that they were one people, the people of one true God. Chosen, called, saved, and disciplined by him for his purposes.

"Honour your father and mother that your days may be long in the land which I will give you." The child snuggled close to his mother in the warmth of the camp-fire, and they knew that they were one family under the fatherhood of one God.

"Do not kill."

"Do not commit adultery."

"Do not steal or bear false witness."

"Do not covet."

Clear demands, clean as the desert and the sun over the desert. There in the fire-light they knew that these laws would make them a mighty nation, and that in the long future they would become the granite foundation of cities and civilizations yet to be born.

The Death of Moses

Israel wandered on from Sinai, and at last after many years they came to the slopes of a mountain called Pisgah.

Moses, now a very old man, frail and withered like an autumn leaf, stood and gazed down at the land spread out beneath him. It was Canaan, the Promised Land, a green chequer-board of forests and fields stretching to the blue line of the Mediterranean on the horizon.

There on the mountain God spoke to Moses for the last time.

"This is the land I promised to Abraham, to Isaac, and to Jacob. With your eyes you have seen it, but you shall not enter it, for your long task is done."

So Moses handed over his leadership to the soldier Joshua, and there on the slopes of Pisgah he died. And to this day no man knows his grave.

Joshua Before Jericho

Joshua led Israel down from Pisgah and across the River Jordan which marked the boundary of Canaan. For the first time the Chosen People stood on the soil of the Promised Land. But before them with grim walls sheer as cliffs lay the city of Jericho guarding the river-crossing. Joshua knew that the city must be stormed before they could invade the land, and he also knew as he looked at the massive fortifications, that it would not be easy.

That night as the army rested by the camp-fires, talking softly of the coming battle, Joshua went apart to a hill where he could gaze down on the beleaguered city. There in the starlight he came face to face with another soldier, alone and fully armed like himself. As Joshua gazed, the stranger seemed to grow before him, until his bulk seemed to fill the sky and his eyes shone like two suns.

"I have come," said the stranger softly, "as the captain of the army of the Lord . . ."

Joshua fell to his knees before the angel and knew no more.

When he came to himself the sky was pale with dawn and he was alone. But he knew what he must do, and he knew that the attack would succeed, for God was indeed with them.

That very morning Joshua led the army out of the camp while the defenders of Jericho stood to their arms on the walls of the city. But the expected attack did not come.

In perfect formation the Israelite army marched across the plain and around the walls. In the middle of the column priests carried the Ark of God containing the stone tablets which Moses had brought down from the mountain. The morning sun flashed on sword and armour and on the gold of the Ark.

In silence they marched. There was not a word, not a song, not a sound except the tramp of marching feet and the eerie wailing of the priests' trumpets.

Round the city they went, and back to the camp. The next day they did the same, and the next. For six whole days this went on. On the seventh day the

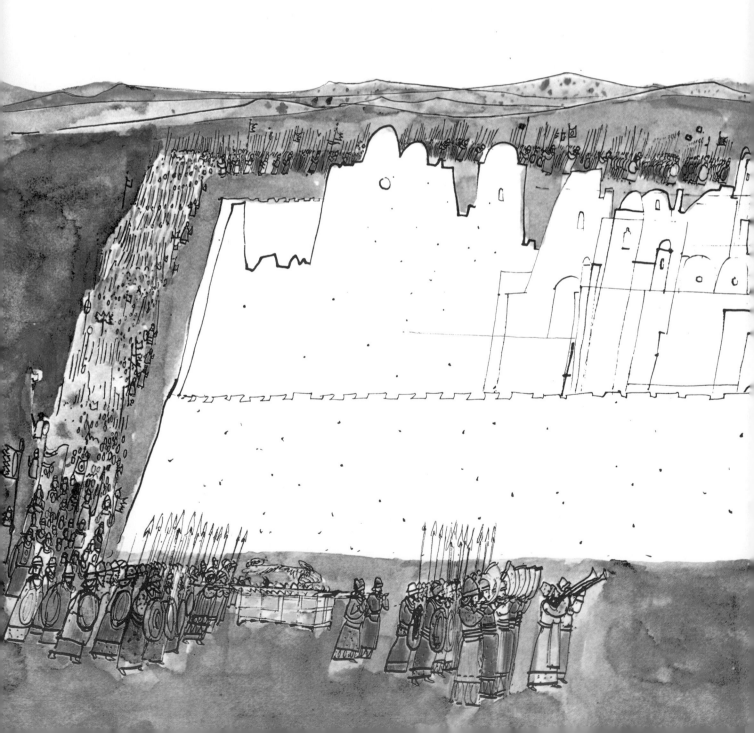

marching column went round the city as before, but this time they went on round again until they had circled the city seven times in total silence except for the fearsome trumpets. Then they all stopped dead and turned inward, a great ring of armed men circling the city. Then with one shattering trumpet-blast they charged for the city wall. In no time they were over the fortifications, and the city was taken. And ever afterwards the Israelites knew that the army of the Lord had indeed fought alongside them on the day that Joshua captured Jericho.

Samson

After the fall of Jericho the Israelites quickly overran the Promised Land, but for many years they had to fight the Philistines for possession. The Philistines were fierce invaders from over the sea who had weapons of iron, better than the bronze of the Israelites. The struggle was long and bitter, and sometimes one nation had the upper hand and sometimes the other.

During these desperate years Israel had many great leaders whom they called Judges.

Samson was one of the most famous of the Judges, and he was certainly the strongest. Once he killed a lion with his bare hands. Once he won a battle with only the jawbone of a donkey for a weapon.

Once he escaped from the Philistine fortress of Gaza carrying away the main gates on his back. But the source of his great strength was a secret between Samson and God.

Now Samson fell in love with a woman called Delilah. She was beautiful but false, and she agreed with the Philistine lords to betray Samson.

"Tell me the secret of your strength, Samson," she pleaded, and went on pleading until he said, "Bind me with seven green twigs of willow. Then my strength will be that of other men."

That night while Samson slept, Delilah bound him with seven green twigs of willow, while the Philistine soldiers waited in the next room.

"The Philistines have come!" she cried. And Samson awoke and snapped the twigs as if they had been cotton. For this was not the secret of his strength.

Again Delilah pleaded, and again Samson relented.

"Bind me with new ropes," he said, "then I shall be as other men."

So while he slept Delilah bound him with new ropes.

"The Philistines have come!" she cried. And Samson awoke and snapped the ropes as if they had been thread. For this was not his secret.

Again she tried.

"Weave the hair of my head in the loom as if it were wool," he said.

So while he slept Delilah wove his hair, moving the loom softly lest he should awake. But when she wakened him with her cry he pulled the beam from the loom with the hair of his head. For neither was this the secret of his strength.

One last time Delilah tried, using all her beauty and all her cunning. This time, because he loved her so, Samson told her the whole truth. "Since I was a child," he said, "my hair has never been cut. For this was the sign that my life was vowed to the God of Israel. This is the source of my strength."

Delilah went to the Philistine lords. "This time he has told me all his heart," she said.

That night while Samson slept she took scissors and cut off all his hair. "The Philistines have come," she cried. And as Samson awoke, his enemies burst in and bound him and took him away to Gaza, where they put out his eyes and treated him as the meanest slave.

In Gaza the Philistine lords held a great feast before their god. They grew merry with wine and shouted for Samson to be brought to make sport for them. Samson came, led by a boy, and they stood him by the two great central pillars which held up the palace.

Blind Samson stood among his enemies and prayed silently to the God of Israel. "O Lord God, remember me this once, I pray thee, and give me back my great strength." Then he set his arms against the two great central pillars and started to push. The pillars trembled, then cracked, then they collapsed, bringing down the whole palace in tumbling ruin, and burying Samson with all the lords of the enemies of Israel.

Samuel in the Temple

The years passed and the Israelites settled in the Promised Land. But they forgot the hardness and simplicity of their life in the desert, the days when they knew that the Lord was the God of Israel. But God would not let them forget altogether. He raised up great men, not warriors like Joshua, but men with far-seeing eyes who could speak of His ways. These men were called prophets, and the first was Samuel.

Samuel was dedicated to the service of God when he was a baby, by his parents. They put him in the care of old Eli the priest who kept the temple of God in Shilo, where the Ark rested now that there was peace.

Eli had two sons, Hophni and Phineas. They helped their father in the ritual of the temple, but unlike their father, they were evil men, cheating the worshippers and extorting money from them.

Samuel slept in the temple itself at night. The lamp which burned before the Ark of God cast great flickering shadows across pillars and roof beams. But Samuel was not afraid. He had always slept on his little bed before the golden Ark. To him it was home.

One night before the sanctuary lamp went out, Samuel lay awake watching the shadows chase one another across the smoky rafters. As he lay, clear across the silent temple he heard his name called: "Samuel!"

Thinking it was old Eli calling, he sprang from his bed and ran across the cold pavement to Eli's room. But Eli said, "I did not call you. Lie down again, my son."

So Samuel went back to his bed. But again his name was called, clear through the darkness: "Samuel!" He ran to Eli, and again the old man sent him back to his bed.

When it happened the third time, with great awe Eli realized that it was God who was calling Samuel.

"Go and lie down," he said. "And if He calls again, say: 'Speak, Lord, your servant is listening.'"

With pounding heart Samuel lay and waited.

"Samuel!" The Lord came and called as before, His voice like a bell in the dark temple.

"Speak, Lord, your servant is listening," replied Samuel.

So the great God who long before had spoken in the wind and on the mountains to the mighty leaders of the past, spoke that night in the stillness of the temple to a little boy lying on his bed.

Samuel did not understand all that God said, but he understood enough to know that the Lord was displeased with Hophni and Phineas for their wicked ways, and that they would come to a bad end—which indeed happened.

Samuel lay until the dawn light was grey at the windows, the words of God ringing in his ears: "The evil that these men do cannot be cleansed by sacrifices." Words which the prophets would say again and again in a hundred different ways down the long centuries to the far-off prophet Micah who one day would cry: "He has showed you, O man, what is good. What does the Lord require of you but to act justly, to love mercy, and to walk humbly with your God?"

Samuel Anoints David as King

Samuel grew up to be a great prophet and leader of his people, when war with the Philistines broke out again.

Through Samuel, God called Saul to be the first king of Israel. He was a great warrior and a giant of a man, head and shoulders taller than other men.

At first Saul was a good king, and he and his son Jonathan had great success in battle. But he turned away from God, and at last God spoke again to Samuel as long ago He had spoken in the temple:

"Go to Bethlehem and anoint as king one of the sons of Jesse."

So Samuel set out for Bethlehem, but for fear of Saul he pretended he was going to make a sacrifice to God.

When he arrived he called Jesse and his seven sons to the sacrifice. He looked at them all carefully, but fine men though they were, he knew that none of them was of God's choosing.

"Are these all your children?" he asked Jesse.

"There is only David, the youngest, left," Jesse replied. "He is tending the sheep."

"Bring him to me!" said Samuel.

When the young man arrived, God's voice spoke in Samuel's heart, and he knew that this was the future king. He took oil, and there in the presence of all his brothers he anointed David king over Israel.

From that day, though they kept the anointing secret until the time was ripe, the Spirit of God departed from Saul and rested on David.

47

David and Goliath

The Philistines had a great warrior, a giant called Goliath. He was so strong, so well armed with his helmet of bronze, his mail coat, and his spear thick as a weaver's beam, that he might have been a match for Samson.

The two armies stood facing each other across a plain, and every morning Goliath strode out and challenged Israel to produce a champion to fight him in single combat. But none dared face him, even though Saul for very desperation had promised his daughter and great riches to anyone who could kill the giant.

Now David came to the camp bearing food for his brothers who were serving with the army. He heard Goliath make his morning challenge and was horrified to see all the soldiers of Israel fall back before the giant like sheep fleeing from a wolf. Scornfully he asked, "Who is this Philistine to defy the armies of the living God?" But his brothers were angry with him and told him to go back to minding sheep and leave the business of war to men.

But David went to the tent of King Saul. "I will go out and fight this Philistine," he said. The king gazed at him in astonishment; a handsome lad, too young to have a beard, and with the light build and swinging stride of the mountaineer. His heart warmed to the boy's courage, despite the ridiculousness of his gay challenge.

"You're only a lad," he said. "He's been a soldier all his life."

"I am a shepherd boy," replied David. "Both a lion and a bear have taken lambs from my flock. Both I hunted, and both I killed. The Lord who protected me from the talon of the lion and the claw of the bear will shield me from this Philistine."

For a long moment they gazed into one another's eyes, the king that was and the king that was to be; the troubled eyes of a great grizzled man, and the frank eyes of a light-limbed youth. Then the king answered, speaking slowly and solemnly as if the Spirit of the Lord was between them: "So be it. And the Lord go with you."

They armed David in the king's own mailed coat and bronze helmet, and they put the king's sword into his hand. David tried a few steps beneath the great weight of the armour.

"No," he said. "I shall get nowhere in these." He took off all the armour, gathered five smooth stones from the stream and put them in his shepherd's pouch, then with his good oaken staff in one hand and his shepherd's sling in the other, he walked lightly out to meet the Philistine who stood alone, massive as a battlemented tower in the empty plain between the armies.

When Goliath saw David he threw back his head so that the bronze helm glittered like the sun itself, and he laughed. How he laughed. Great rumbling belly laughter like tumbling rocks sounding across the plain. "Am I a dog," he roared, "that you come with a stick? Come to me"—he beckoned with a finger like a bull's horn—"Come to me, little one, and I will feed your flesh to the crows."

David stood a few yards away from the giant, just out of range of that enormous spear, and defied him, his clear voice like the sound of music singing across the plain: "Goliath, you come with sword and spear and shield. But I come armed with the name of the Lord, the God of Israel. Today He will deliver you into my hand. I am going to kill you, Goliath. I am going to kill you, and both these armies will know that the salvation of the Lord God is not to be won with sword and spear."

With a great roar the Philistine charged at David. But the light-footed shepherd side-stepped the lumbering giant, as a mountain cat would evade the charge of a bull. Swiftly he fitted a stone to his sling, and as the heavily armed Philistine turned to face him again, he hurled it.

Straight the stone flew, like an arrow to a target. It hit the giant square between the eyes just below the futile protection of the helmet.

Goliath stood for a moment, motionless as if in surprise; then, as a big tree falls, slowly at first but at last with an earth-shaking crash, so the giant collapsed from the knees and lay still upon the plain like the ruins of a castle keep.

With a shout of triumph the army of Israel broke their watching ranks and came pouring across the plain to the astonished Philistines.

So the day ended with a great victory for Israel, and when they returned from the pursuit, Abner, the general of Saul's army, took David to the king that he might enter Saul's service. So the king who was to be, knelt before the king who still wore the crown, swore allegiance to him and became his armour-bearer.

The Sweet Singer of Israel

David and Saul's son Jonathan became firm friends, so that in after years men linked their names together when they wished to talk of friendship. With Jonathan and David vying with one another in acts of daring, the army of Saul won many victories. But one day as the army returned triumphant, Saul heard the crowd singing a new ballad of welcome—

> "Saul has killed his thousands,
> And David his ten thousands."

From that day Saul hated David. A prey to dark jealousies, deserted by the Spirit of God, he became a man sick in mind. Only music could help him when the black fit was upon him, and best of all was the music of David who was the finest harper and poet in Israel.

Saul would sit alone in his hall and David would sing the old songs of his people. Songs of the years in the desert and of the great escape from Egypt. He would sing of the glory of God as maker of all things, of the beauty and majesty of God's love for his people, and of the Law clean as the desert sun searching the crannies of the rock. But best of all he would remember—perhaps with longing —the simple days of the past when he had been a shepherd.

"The Lord is my shepherd; I shall not want.
He maketh me to lie down in green pastures: he leadeth me
beside the still waters."

Then he would remember the dangers of the shepherd's life, the bear and the lion lurking in dark places.

"Yea, though I walk through the valley of the shadow of death,
I will fear no evil: for thou art with me; thy rod and thy staff
they comfort me."

So David would sing and King Saul's sickness would be a little eased.
And in after years when men collected together all the old songs of Israel and put them in a book, they called the book after the sweet singer of Israel: "The Psalms of David."

David and Jonathan

Saul's jealousy against David grew. One day, as they sat together in the great hall, Saul's dark broodings came to a sudden head. Without warning he seized his javelin and hurled it at David, and it was only David's quickness of movement that saved his life.

David fled from the court, but Jonathan followed him and found him where he was hiding in the wilderness. Together they laid a plan so that they should know what Saul really intended and whether it was safe for David to return to court.

David remained in hiding until the new moon, when there was a religious festival with a banquet at which as Saul's armour-bearer David should have been present.

The new moon came and the king sat in his place in the great hall. All the courtiers were there in their places, except David.

"Where is the son of Jesse?" asked the king.

Jonathan replied, "I gave him permission, my Lord, to go to Bethlehem for a family sacrifice."

Saul's terrible anger flared against his own son.

"As long as David lives," he thundered, "you will never be king. Bring him to me that I may kill him."

"Why?" cried Jonathan. "What has he done?"

But Saul replied only with his javelin, hurling it at his son as he had hurled it at David.

Jonathan took his bow, and with his squire went down to where David was hiding. He shot the arrows and sent the young man to find them, shouting after him words which David in his hiding-place knew were words of exile: "Go farther. The arrows are beyond you." And then for very urgency Jonathan added, "Make haste. Do not stay."

But because he could not bear to part so with his friend, Jonathan sent his squire back to the city, and David came out of his hiding-place. The two strong men embraced one another and wept like children, so great was their love.

"Go in peace," said Jonathan. "Let us remember the friendship between us which we swore before the Lord."

So David went into exile, and Jonathan returned slowly to the city.

David in Exile

In exile David gathered about him a band of outlaws, and they had a stronghold in the desert called Adullam. Many were the adventures David and his men had. Many raids they made, and often Saul sought for his enemy but he never penetrated Adullam.

It was a good fortress, secret and well defended. But it was a harsh and rocky place, a place of fierce sun and little water. Often David longed for the green hills of his boyhood home around Bethlehem. But Bethlehem was in the hands of the Philistines.

One day, as David yearned for peace and the cool of home, he said to himself —but out loud: "Bethlehem. The well of Bethlehem in the twilight. Oh, that someone would bring me water from the well of Bethlehem."

Three of his comrades overheard, and that night they slipped out of Adullam and across the moonlit countryside to Bethlehem.

Over the wall they went, and before the guard was roused they were away again like shadows in the night.

They came to David and held out their gift, shyly like boys.

"Water. From the well of Bethlehem," they said.

But David would not drink it. He poured it out on the altar of the God of Israel.

"O Lord," he said, "accept this offering. It is the blood of my comrades who went in jeopardy of their lives."

57

David Comes to the Throne

Because the Lord was no longer with Saul, the Philistines overran the land. Old, sick, and desperate as he faced one last battle, Saul turned once again to the necromancy which in his better days he had forbidden. He went to Endor where there was a famous witch, and by dark of night he came to her cottage.

"Mother," he said as they sat by the light of the fire, "use your art. Call up for me the soul of one who is dead."

"It is forbidden," she said. But Saul reassured her.

"Whom shall I recall from the land of shades?" she asked.

"Samuel," whispered Saul as the embers dropped in the hearth and the red light flickered in the dark room.

With the pot and the herbs and the terrible words the witch worked her enchantment.

"I see spirits ascending out of the earth," she cried in a high voice. Saul buried his face in his cloak for he knew that the grey shape flickering before him was the ghost of Samuel. But Samuel's spirit brought no comfort to the king.

"Tomorrow the Lord will deliver Israel into the hand of the Philistines. Tomorrow you and your sons will be with me."

The thin voice sighed into silence, and then there was only the old witch with King Saul stretched unconscious across the hearth.

58

On the morrow so it was. Israel broke before the Philistines as a sand-castle breaks before the sea. Saul was killed, and Jonathan, and all his sons.

David, when they brought the news to him, wrote a lament for them. For Saul, because he had been a king and a mighty warrior. For Jonathan, because he had loved him:

"Saul and Jonathan were lovely and pleasant in their lives,
  and in their death they were not divided:
  They were swifter than eagles, they were stronger than lions . . .
  I am distressed for thee, my brother Jonathan . . .
  Thy love to me was wonderful, passing the love of women.
  How are the mighty fallen, and the weapons of war perished!"

And the people anointed David as king.

Solomon the Magnificent

David reigned for many years, and when he died the kingdom passed to his son Solomon.

In Solomon's reign all the old promises seemed for a brief moment to come true. The Philistines had finally been defeated, Jerusalem had become the capital, and the borders of Israel stretched wider than they would ever stretch again. So that, in later, sadder times men never tired of looking back to the golden age of wise King Solomon.

It was indeed for his wisdom that Solomon was chiefly remembered. One night God appeared in a dream to the young king and asked him what gift he would most like to have. Solomon asked for wisdom to rule well. And the choice

was pleasing to God, so that Solomon was given not only wisdom, but also honour and great riches.

So it was. Solomon married the daughter of great Pharaoh king of Egypt, where once Israel had been enslaved. He filled Jerusalem with new buildings; a palace for Pharaoh's daughter, a temple for the Ark. Palace and temple he filled with precious wood from Tyre, and cast brasswork, and cups and plates of fine gold from Ophir.

He built a navy: quinqueremes, galleys with oars like five-storied houses to bring across the sea the treasures of far countries: ivory, apes, and peacocks, spices and jewels, and the gold of Ophir.

The fabled Queen of Sheba visited Solomon, bringing a long camel train of costly gifts. She was overawed by his magnificence. "What was told me was but half the truth," she said. "Happy your men, happy your servants, and blessed is the Lord your God who set you on the throne of Israel."

In all Solomon's long reign there was peace in Israel. As men said in after years: "Every man dwelt safely, each under his own vine and his own fig-tree from Dan in the far north to Beer-Sheba which marches by the realm of great Pharaoh himself."

Elijah and the Prophets of Baal

Civil war followed Solomon's death and the kingdom was split in two, one part taking the name of Judah and the other part still called Israel.

Ahab, king of Israel, married a beautiful foreign princess called Jezebel. When she moved to Ahab's capital city, Samaria, she brought with her the worship of her own god, Baal. Once she was established as queen she set about promoting the worship of Baal, pulling down the altars of the God of Israel, and hunting and killing his priests and prophets.

The word of God came to Elijah in the hill country of Gilead. A wild and rugged figure with long hair, Elijah, called by God, faced Ahab in his gleaming new capital city.

"As the Lord God of Israel lives," cried Elijah, pointing an accusing finger at the king, "for the evil that is done in this land there shall be neither dew nor rain until by the word of the Lord in my mouth the rain comes again."

He stalked from the city. Led by the Spirit of God, he went eastward and hid by the brook Cherith. He drank from the brook while drought struck the land behind him. And God caused the ravens to feed him so that he should not starve.

The drought went on and the brook Cherith dried up. Led by the Spirit, Elijah went to Sarepta where he stayed with a widow. And all the time he lived with her, God provided meal in the barrel and oil in the cruse so that they should not starve. Meanwhile in Israel grim famine marched on the heels of drought.

At last God spoke to Elijah: "Go to Ahab. Do what I shall show you. Then I will send rain on the earth."

Elijah stood before Ahab, and the king said, "You have come, you destroyer of Israel."

"It is you who have destroyed Israel," replied Elijah. "You have forsaken the Lord and followed Baal. But let us now see once and for all, who is the true God."

They gathered all Israel on Mount Carmel. Ahab was there and four hundred and fifty of the prophets of Baal. Elijah stood in the middle of that great assembly.

64

"How long will you halt between two opinions?" he cried. "If the Lord is God, follow Him, but if Baal, then follow Baal."

They erected two altars, one for each god. The wood was cut, the sacrifice prepared, but they did not light the fires.

"Now," shouted Elijah to the prophets of Baal, "call on your god. The god who sends fire to kindle the sacrifice, let him be Lord."

A fierce rumble of assent rose from the listening throng.

The prophets of Baal called on their god from dawn until noon.

"Shout louder," mocked Elijah. "Perhaps he is out hunting. Perhaps he has fallen asleep." The prophets cried and shouted, they lashed themselves into a frenzy of ceremonial dancing and cut themselves with knives until the sun slanted down into the sea. But Baal did not answer, and at last his prophets sank exhausted to the ground.

A great hush came over the mountainside, and the evening was calm. "Come near to me," said Elijah to all the people, and his voice was gentle for so fierce a man. He made them fetch water and drench the sacrifice on the altar of the Lord. Then alone he stood before the altar, and at the time of the evening sacrifice in Solomon's temple he prayed, his voice calm on the evening breeze.

"Lord God of Abraham, of Isaac, and of Israel, let it be known this day that thou art God."

Instantly the fire fell from heaven like lightning, like a thunderbolt, and the smoke of the sacrifice rose, a black line across the evening sky. With one accord the people knelt. "The Lord is God," they cried. "The Lord is God."

Elijah left them kneeling, and alone, except for his servant, he climbed to the summit of Carmel. There he knelt and prayed. Then he said to his servant, "Go and look westward over the sea."

The man returned. "I saw nothing," he said.

Seven times this happened, and the last time the servant returned and said, "I saw a cloud arise out of the sea. A cloud no bigger than a man's hand." And as Ahab drove away from Carmel, that night there was a great storm of wind and rain.

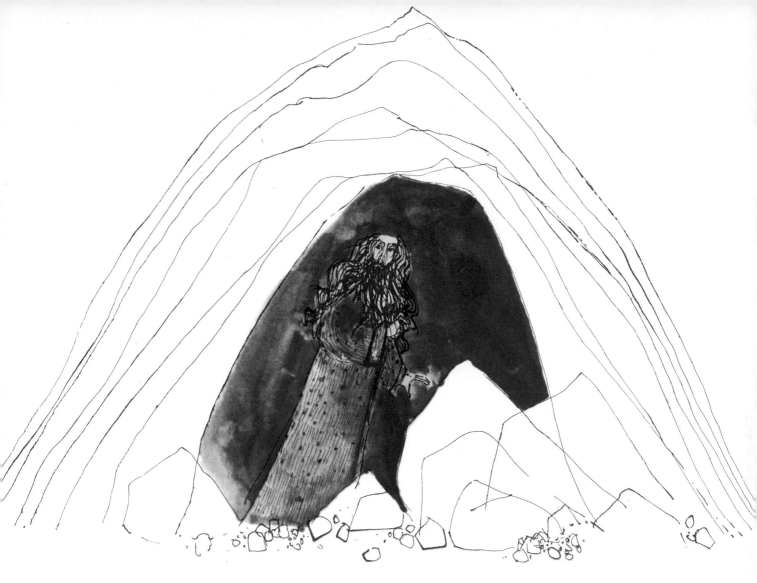

Elijah and the Still, Small Voice

Jezebel hunted Elijah and he fled for his life to Horeb, the mountain of God where the Lord had spoken to Moses from the burning bush.

Elijah hid in a cave, and as he lay there he said bitterly, "All the prophets are dead. The people have forsaken the Covenant. Only I am left, and they seek my life."

There was a great wind on the mountainside. But Elijah knew that God was not in the wind. After the wind an earthquake rocked the ground, but God was not in the earthquake. Then lightning and fire from heaven flickered around the mountain. But God was not in these. After the fire there was silence, and in the silence a still, small voice, like the voice that had called Samuel in the temple. Elijah wrapped his mantle about him and stood in the cave mouth. He told God all his fears and all his bitterness, and the still, small voice told him what he must do.

"Do not be afraid," it ended. "I have yet seven thousand in Israel who have not bowed in worship to Baal."

Isaiah

In the north there arose a great military power called Assyria, and in Jerusalem and Samaria men's hearts failed them for fear. In Jerusalem there lived a man called Isaiah. One day he went into Solomon's temple, and there he saw a vision.

"I saw," he wrote afterwards, "the Lord sitting upon a throne high and lifted up, and His train filled the temple. Around Him stood angels, the seraphim. And one cried to another: 'Holy, holy, holy is the Lord of hosts; the whole earth is full of His glory.'"

Isaiah crouched down, blinded by the presence, and from His throne the Lord spoke.

"Whom shall I send?" cried the great voice. "Who will go for us?" And Isaiah heard his own voice reply, "Here am I. Send me."

So Isaiah learned that the God of his fathers would speak through his lips in the terrible time of danger that lay ahead.

The Assyrian army descended on Israel like wolves. Samaria was besieged and at last fell. The people of Israel, ten of the original twelve tribes, were led away into slavery, and to this day no man knows what became of them.

In Jerusalem the king of Judah turned to Egypt for help against the invaders. Isaiah warned him what would happen.

"Sennacherib, king of Assyria, will come," he said, "and lay siege against the city of David."

And so it proved. One after another, like card castles before the wind, the fortresses of Judah fell before the Assyrian army. The king tried to buy off Sennacherib with all his own treasure and all the gold and silver from Solomon's temple. But it was useless. Heralds of the Assyrian army arrived before the barred gates of Jerusalem.

"In whom do you trust?" they shouted arrogantly to the watchers on the wall. "In Egypt—that broken reed? Have any of the gods delivered their lands out of the hand of mighty Sennacherib? Open the gates. Otherwise Jerusalem shall be destroyed."

The watchers told the king what the heralds had said, and he went alone into the stripped temple to pray.

"O Lord God," he prayed. "Save us from Sennacherib, that all the earth may know that you alone are God."

As he rose from his knees there came a message from Isaiah.

"God has heard your prayer. Tell Sennacherib that the daughter of Zion defies him. He shall not come into this city, for I will defend it for my sake and my servant David's sake."

So in the power of the Lord the king sent his defiance to Sennacherib and prepared to defend Jerusalem to the end.

But the Assyrian army never came. Some say that on the same night the angel of death visited their camp and slew by thousands. Some say that Sennacherib heard a rumour of rebellion at home.

Whatever the cause, that night he turned from the Holy City and went home. Twenty years later he was murdered by his own sons as he worshipped Nisroch his god in the temple at Nineveh.

Jeremiah

The great power of Assyria was over-thrown by an even more terrible tyranny, Babylon. Once again Judah was invaded, and as in former years, God called a prophet to speak for Him in the time of trial, a man called Jeremiah. Jeremiah's message was not a popular one:

"You must submit to Babylon. Otherwise the kingdom will be overrun and Jerusalem destroyed."

Judah was invaded, and Jerusalem surrounded by the iron regiments of Babylon. Jeremiah's message never varied: "Submit!"

So although Zedekiah the king did his best to protect Jeremiah, there were many among the garrison who considered that he was nothing but a traitor.

One day, unknown to Zedekiah, his enemies had Jeremiah arrested. They took him and hurled him into an empty water-cistern, a pit cut into the rock upon which the fortress was built. They dragged the stone cover over the entrance and left him there to die.

Jeremiah lay in the mud at the bottom of the cistern. The footfall of his captors echoed away into silence above his head, and there was only the drip and drop of water in a darkness deep as that of the Egyptian plague.

As he waited for the death which must surely come, Jeremiah thought back over his life and his dealings with the God whom he had tried to serve. Was he being deserted by God? Had all the promises which had haunted his people since Abraham had first answered God's call, come to nothing?

"Your children shall be numberless as the stars of the night sky, and in your seed shall all the nations of the earth be blessed." That had been the promise, and it had all come to this: Jerusalem beleaguered and the last of the prophets dying in a black hole. Yet despite it all, Jeremiah still trusted God.

Then in the darkness God told him the answer. As David had said long ago when he fought Goliath, God's salvation did not come with spear and sword. Great words, words winged like angels, shifted and arranged themselves in Jeremiah's mind.

"Thus says the Lord, I will bring my people again to this place. I will make a new Covenant. I will put my law in their minds, and I will write it in their hearts, and I will be their God and they shall be my people."

Even as Jeremiah thought this, there was a scrape and a bump over his head as the cover was taken off the pit and the blessed daylight flooded in. King Zedekiah had heard what had been done to Jeremiah, and had sent men with ropes to lift him out of the pit.

So Jeremiah was able to write down his vision of a new sort of kingdom which did not depend on strength of arms. And when, as he had foretold, Jerusalem was destroyed, the long lines of slaves took a new hope with them into captivity; the hope that one day they would return, but that however far off that day might be, God was not tied to temple or territory but was with them always in their minds and in their hearts.

By the Waters of Babylon

For the Children of Israel life in Babylon was not as bad as they had expected. Life went on and they settled down. They got jobs. They married. They built houses. But always they kept themselves separate from their captors because of the truths about God which they had learned in their long story. And always they remembered with longing the Promised Land from which they had been exiled, and the ruined city of David where the owl nested in the broken tower and the jackal called beneath the moon in the empty street.

One of their poets wrote of it:

"By the waters of Babylon, we sat down and wept: when we remembered thee, O Zion.

As for our harps, we hanged them up: upon the trees that are therein.

For they that led us away captive required of us then a song, and melody in our heaviness: Sing us one of the songs of Zion.

How shall we sing the Lord's song: in a strange land?"

In after years they did go back, led by a soldier called Nehemiah. They restored Jerusalem and rebuilt the wall, labouring with mason's trowel in one hand and spear in the other. They brought back from Babylon many of the treasures which had been stolen from the temple. But more than this they brought a clearer idea of God and a new hope which had grown out of their own suffering.

They who had seen so much war and bloodshed now knew that God's kingdom would never be ushered in with spear and sword. It would come out of suffering, won by a man who would suffer, and so establish God's rule in the hearts and minds of men.

One of the prophets who was with them in Babylon wrote about it:

"He is despised and rejected of men; a man of sorrows, and acquainted with grief. . . .
But he was wounded for our transgressions, he was bruised for our iniquities . . . and with his stripes we are healed."

THE NEW TESTAMENT

The Birth of Jesus

The power of Babylon waned like that of Assyria and Egypt and there arose a new empire—Rome, greatest of all empires. Rome ruled the world, holding all the nations in the iron grip of the legions.

Word went out from Rome that for tax reasons all men must return to the places of their birth in order to register their names. So one night two people, Joseph and Mary, came slowly into the little town of Bethlehem.

Joseph had come to Bethlehem because he was a descendant of King David. He had brought Mary with him because she was soon to have a baby, and he did not want to leave her alone in Nazareth where he was the village carpenter.

At twilight they came to the inn near the well in the village square. But because of all the travellers there was no room in the inn, so they had to use the stable for want of a better place. There in the stable Mary had her baby, and because she had no cot she laid him in the hay in the manger from which the cattle fed.

So Bethlehem slept, except for the shepherds up on the hills. They were guarding their flocks from wolves under a frosty sky where the stars were like a million holes in blue velvet. Suddenly in the sky there was a great light, and in the light great shapes, winged creatures—angels. The shepherds were very frightened and cowered down by their pale camp-fire. Then came the voice and the singing—or perhaps the voice and the singing were one. Certainly they were beautiful and not of this earth.

"Good news," sang the voice. "Today in David's city a deliverer has been born for you—the Messiah, the Lord. This is the sign: a baby lying in a manger."

The voice and the singing ceased and the heavens closed. For all its stars the night sky seemed to the shepherds dull as muddy water, and the bright camp-fire grey as ashes on a cold hearth.

As soon as they came to themselves, the shepherds hurried down to Bethlehem, leaving the dogs to guard the sheep. They walked through the sleeping town. They came to the inn and found the stable. There in the manger was the baby called Jesus, Joseph kneeling beside him, Mary sitting by his head as he slept in peace.

The shepherds crept across the rustling straw, and then they knelt and gazed at the baby. Partly they worshipped, and partly they wondered—the very first of the countless millions who have done exactly the same.

So there was peace in the stable. And outside, all the people in the little town slept, unaware of the great thing that had happened. And up on the hills, the dogs lay with their heads on their paws, watchful for fear of danger.

The Wise Men

In a far country, many days' journey to the east of Palestine, an astrologer gazed from a high tower at the night sky. Low in the west, like white fire on the horizon beyond the desert, burned a star. By his art, with astrolabe and rare books and a chart of the heavens, he calculated that the star was herald of the birth of one favoured of the gods, a king or saviour. In haste he came down from his tower, in haste he ordered the fitting-out of an expedition and the saddling of camels.

When the red disc of the sun inched over the city behind him, his moving shadow was long like an arrow pointing westward before him, swinging with the swinging stride of the camels toward whatever wonders lay over the horizon.

No man knows how long was his journey over the shifting sand. But he came out of the east, and when he arrived in the Promised Land he had companions, lords and astrologers like himself, who had also seen the wonderful star.

The wise men, as was to be expected from such great lords, went straight to the palace of the king in Jerusalem. For he, after all, could be expected to know of the birth of a great one. Now the king was called Herod, and he held his throne not in his own right, but by permission of Rome.

Lords with such a retinue were granted immediate audience. They strode into Herod's audience-chamber, magnificent and strange with their dark faces and their rich oriental robes.

"Great king," cried the spokesman, bowing low before Herod, "where is the child who is born to be king of the Jews? We observed the rising of his star and have come from afar to pay him homage."

Herod was much alarmed by this talk of a king, but he was far too cunning to show it. With smooth words and gracious hospitality he turned aside the question. But no sooner were the wise men out of the audience-chamber, than Herod summoned all the chief priests and scholars wise in the law and history of Israel.

"In the ancient writings of Israel," he said as they stood around his throne, "it is recorded that one day a king and saviour will be born. One who will bear your griefs and carry your sorrows. One through whom all the nations of the earth shall be blessed."

84

"The Messiah," they said.

Herod nodded. "Where will he be born?" He asked the question casually.

"In Bethlehem in Judaea," they replied. "For it says in the Scriptures: 'Bethlehem, you are far from the least in Judah. Out of you shall come a leader, the shepherd of my people Israel.' "

Herod nodded again, and concealing a pretended yawn as if the whole subject suddenly bored him, he dismissed them.

Next morning he saw the wise men in private. "I trust you are rested," he said. They thanked him with oriental courtesy for his hospitality. Herod bowed in courtly acknowledgement and then: "The one whom you seek," he said, "his birth is expected in Bethlehem, an insignificant village in Judaea. Go there. If you find him, bring me word . . ." He paused and examined his finger-nails. ". . . Bring me word. I should like to do him homage myself."

At the king's bidding the wise men set out. They came to Bethlehem, and
there they found Mary and Joseph and the baby Jesus. They came into the house
where they were lodging, and bending the knee, they did grave homage to the
unknowing child while his mother and Joseph gazed in wonder. Then with
courtly bows to Mary they withdrew, leaving rich presents: gold because the
star had heralded a king; incense because they had looked for a priest; myrrh
which is used for burials because the scriptures said the Messiah must suffer.

86

They slept that night in Bethlehem before returning to Jerusalem. And in the night one of them dreamed that Herod was a wolf who would destroy the lamb, the infant Messiah. In the morning he told his dream to his companions, and taking it for a sign, they avoided Jerusalem and set out eastward, homeward across the desert.

A few days later Joseph also dreamed. In his dream an angel appeared and warned him that Herod would try to kill Jesus. He awoke tossing on his bed, with sweat on his brow and the word "Egypt" on his lips. So without more ado he saddled the donkey and set out with Mary and Jesus for the kingdom of the Nile.

It was as well he did. Herod's anger was terrible when he realized that the wise men had tricked him. He sent a troop of soldiers with orders to murder every child under two years old in Bethlehem and the surrounding countryside. The terrible massacre was carried out while, all unknowing, Joseph, Mary and Jesus were making their slow way southward to Egypt.

So, by the hand of God, the Saviour was saved from the enmity of Herod, and Jesus lived safe in Egypt until Herod died. Then Joseph set out for home, and at last came back to Nazareth and rubbed the rust off his tools, and found that the village was glad to have its carpenter back again.

Jesus' Baptism

For hundreds of years there had been no prophets in Israel. Suddenly, mysteriously, out of the desert came John, a man whom they called "The Baptist" because of his message. He was a wild figure, with his skin dried by the sun like old leather, and wearing a robe woven from camel hair.

"Repent," he cried in a voice like doom. "Be washed clean of your sins by baptism here in the River Jordan, for the Kingdom of God knocks at the very door."

Priests, tradesmen, fat, respectable citizens from Jerusalem, they flocked to John as he preached on the banks of the Jordan.

"Are you the Messiah, the saviour of Israel?" they asked.

"I am a voice," he shouted, the wind whipping his unkempt hair. "Nothing but a voice crying in the wilderness: 'Prepare the way of the Lord.' There is one coming whose shoe I am not worthy to unlace. Repent and be baptized."

90

There came a day when Jesus, now grown to manhood, laid aside his plane and set out from Nazareth. He came to the River Jordan where John was baptizing. He took his turn with the people waiting and at last faced John. Thigh-deep in the river they gazed at one another.

"You come to me," said John at last. "But I have need to come to you."

"Even so," Jesus replied. "But you and I must do all that God requires."

So there in the River Jordan, Jesus was baptized by John. And at that moment, as men said afterwards, the heavens opened and a voice spoke:

"This is my beloved Son."

Jesus is Tempted

After leaving John, Jesus went into the desert to think about his future. There under the sun temptation came to him as long before it had come to Eve.

The desert is harsh, and hunger clawed like a beast at his stomach. With the hunger came a tempting voice, not like God's voice. More like the serpent's voice which Eve heard in the Garden of Eden. "The Son of God? Indeed! Here is a stone—turn it into bread."

"Scripture says," Jesus replied, "man lives not only by bread, but by God's word." Like a shadow on the sun the temptation passed.

The desert moon was cold on the rock, and Jesus was alone on one of the high pinnacles of the temple. Below him flat roofs, silver domes, black lines of alleys, where all the city slept. It was still and silent, only a dog barked in the far hills. Temptation came like a bat's wing across the moon.

"The Son of God? Prove it. Jump. God's angels will hold you up—David said so in the Scripture."

"But the Scripture also says, 'Do not tempt God'," Jesus replied. The shadow passed and the moon was clear.

Jesus was on a high mountain; like Sinai, or Mont Blanc, or Everest. It was a high place of the mind from which he could see all the earth from the beginning to the end of time: Adam in the garden, Solomon in Jerusalem, the hanging gardens of Babylon, the white pillars of imperial Rome, skyscrapers in New York, motor-cars in London, and pinnacles like onions in Moscow. But all this was only like a backdrop in a theatre. Across all the cities there marched armies. There was the cry of victory and the acclamation of heroes. Kings were crowned, poets honoured, ordinary people laughed and cried, and suffered and died.

Out of this pageant of all the kingdoms of all the world came the temptation: "All this shall be yours—if you will kneel and worship me."

"No!" said Jesus. "Be gone, Satan. It is written, you shall worship only God."

The vision faded. Jesus was alone. The heat haze shimmered over the desert, the lizard flicked across the burning rock.

94

In the Storm

Jesus gathered around him twelve friends called disciples. They went about together proclaiming a new message: "The time has come. The Kingdom of God has arrived."

People flocked to Jesus, not only to hear his message but because of his wonderful powers of healing. He cured the blind, the deaf and the dumb, cripples, and those who were sick in mind as well as in body.

One evening, tired from all the demands of the day, he set off with his disciples in a little boat across the Lake of Galilee, making for solitude on the far shore. It was calm and peaceful in the setting sun. But not for long. A sudden squall came storming down from the encircling hills, lashing the placid lake into menacing waves which nearly swamped the boat. The disciples understood their danger, for they were fishermen. Frantically they bailed while Jesus slept on in the stern. But it was no use. Peter, one of the disciples, shook Jesus roughly by the shoulder.

"Master, we're sinking," he shouted in the screaming wind.

Jesus awoke. He stood in the tossing boat, his hair and his clothes flying like flags in the storm. "Hush," he cried into the eye of the wind. "Be still!"

From a shriek the wind dropped to a sigh; from a sigh to a sob; from a sob to stillness. Then there was only the slow toss of the spent waves, and the shipped water slopping in the bottom of the boat.

"Who is he?" whispered the disciples. "Even the wind and sea obey him."

96

The Healer

The far shore of the Lake of Galilee was a lonely, rocky place used only for burials. Among the tombs there lived a poor man who was sick in his mind. He was dangerous, strong and violent, and he wandered in rags, muttering endlessly with the devils in his sick mind, and clanking the chains with which men had tried to bind him.

He met Jesus as the boat grounded on the beach.

"What do you want, Jesus, Son of God?" he babbled.

"What is your name?" Jesus asked.

For a moment the man was almost sane.

"My name is . . ." he began. But then his face and voice changed as the madness took him. "My name is Legion. There are so many of us." He chuckled idiotically.

On the hill-side there was a herd of pigs feeding. The poor man looked wildly round. "Do not cast us out," he pleaded. "Do not cast us into the void. Send us into the pigs."

Gravely Jesus gave his permission. Perhaps pursued by the madman, perhaps indeed possessed by some spirit of evil, the pigs ran in terror down the hill-side and over the cliff.

When the owners of the pigs came from the village, they found their herd destroyed, and the man who had been mad, clean and clothed and sitting contentedly at Jesus' feet.

They were frightened and angry at their loss and begged Jesus to leave their district. So with little rest, Jesus and his disciples went back across the lake. But the man was cured, and a man's soul is worth many animals.

The Forgiver of Sins

Jesus was teaching in the single room of a house with a flat roof. The room was crowded and the street outside was thronged with people struggling to see Jesus.

99

Suddenly, over Jesus' head, there came a thumping and a bumping, and a thin shower of dust fell from the ceiling. Everyone looked up. Lumps started to fall out of the ceiling, and soon there was a hole showing the blue sky, and with four cheerful faces peering over the ragged edge. Then down through the hole came a man on a stretcher supported by ropes held by the man's four friends who were determined that he should see Jesus—even if it did mean knocking a hole in someone else's roof.

Jesus looked at the man on the stretcher.

"Son," he said softly, "your sins are forgiven."

But there were those in the crowd who whispered, "Blasphemy. Make a note of it. Who can forgive sins but God?"

As if he had heard them, Jesus asked a question: "Is it easier to say, 'Your sins are forgiven,' or to say to this poor man, 'Get up and walk'?"

He challenged them with his eyes. But no one dared answer.

"You must learn," he said, "that I, the Son of Man, have power to forgive sins." Then to the paralysed man he said, "Get up. Roll up your stretcher. Go home."

There was a terrible pause. The man struggled to his feet and stood, filled with wonder in the midst of the silent crowd. He rolled up the stretcher and walked stiffly at first like someone who has just laid aside a crutch. The crowd parted before him like traffic before an ambulance. With the stretcher over his shoulder he went out of the door and singing down the street.

The Teacher

Wherever he went Jesus taught people about the Kingdom of God. It is like a grain of mustard seed, he said, like a woman sweeping a room, like a candle in a candle-stick, like a city on a hill. Simple illustrations taken from everyday life. But men said that no one before had ever taught as he did.

Once a lawyer asked him, "What must I do to inherit eternal life?"

"What does the Law say?" asked Jesus in reply.

"Love God with all your heart," quoted the lawyer, "and your neighbour as yourself."

"Do this and you will live," Jesus replied.

But the lawyer was not easily put off. "Who is my neighbour?" he asked.

"Once upon a time," said Jesus, "there was a man travelling from Jerusalem to Jericho. He was attacked by bandits. They beat him up, stripped him, and left him half-dead in the gutter. Then a priest came along the road. He saw the man lying there—and walked on. Next a lawyer came along—and he hurried past in the same way. Last there came a Samaritan who got off his donkey, bound up the man's wounds, and carried him to the nearest inn. Next day he gave money to the landlord. 'Take good care of him,' he said. 'If it costs more than that, I'll make up the difference next time I'm this way.'"

Jesus looked at the lawyer.

"Now," he asked, "which of those three was neighbour to the man who was robbed?"

There was only one possible answer: "The one who showed mercy." Jesus smiled. "Go and do as he did," he said.

"Who is this Jesus?" The question passed from mouth to mouth in the alleys and bazaars of Jerusalem. Everyone discussed it, and not least the disciples.

One day they were speculating about it as they walked along a dusty lane a few paces behind their Master. Suddenly, over his shoulder, Jesus broke into their conversation.

"Who do they say the Son of Man is?"

"John the Baptist come back to life," said one. "Elijah come again," said another. "—Or Jeremiah, or any of the prophets," broke in a third.

"And you?" asked Jesus. "Who do you say I am?"

There was only the sound of their sandals on the road and the humming of the bees in the summer hedgerow. Then with an eagerness all his own, Simon, closest of the disciples, blurted across the silence, "You are the Messiah, the Son of the living God."

Jesus stopped there in the road. Long and lovingly he looked at the sturdy fisherman.

"Simon," he said, "that came to you from my Father. And I say this—you are Peter—the Rock. On this rock I will build, and the forces of death shall never destroy my building."

Jesus, Moses, and Elijah

Six days later Jesus, taking only his closest friends—Simon called Peter, James, and John—went away to be alone with God. All through the long day they climbed up the side of a high mountain, for had not Abraham, and Moses and Elijah met God in the solitude of a mountain?

At the top, with all Israel spread like a map below them, Jesus left his friends to rest and went aside to pray.

As they watched him and wondered, a great change seemed to come over him. He was surrounded by a bright light so that his clothes shone with a whiteness like snow in the sunlight. In the brightness there moved the shapes of two other men. It was Moses, father of the Law, and Elijah, greatest of all the prophets. There on the mountainside they were speaking with Jesus.

Peter broke in, hardly knowing what he said.

"Master, we'll make shelters here on the mountain. So that we can all stay here always."

Even as he spoke there came the shadow of a cloud swooping along the mountainside, and down the piping wind came a voice:

"This is my Son, my beloved. Listen to him."

Then the cloud was gone and the voice was silent. The light faded and the disciples were alone with Jesus on the bleak mountainside. As they came down Jesus reminded them of what the Scriptures said—that the Son of Man must endure great suffering.

Palm Sunday

Despite warnings that evil men were seeking his life, Jesus set out for Jerusalem to celebrate the Passover—the great feast in memory of Israel's escape from Egypt under Moses.

As he came near to the city, riding on a borrowed donkey, he was met by a great crowd.

"Hosanna," they cried. "Three cheers for the Son of David. Blessed is he who

comes in the name of the Lord."

As he came to the city gate the crowds hurled palm-branches before him in the roadway—a green carpet of welcome as the donkey carried him into the city of David.

But his enemies watched the welcome, and they resolved that he must die lest one who was welcomed as David's son should claim David's throne.

Good Friday

Jesus knew that his enemies were plotting his death. He told his disciples so when they met to celebrate the Passover Supper.

During the supper he took bread, broke it, and gave it to them. "This is my body," he said, "which is broken for you! Do this in remembrance of me."

Strange words, but stranger were to follow.

"You will all desert me," he said, "and one of you will betray me."

"I will never desert you," said Peter stoutly.

"You will," replied Jesus sadly. "Before the cock crows you will say three times that you never even knew me."

They went out from supper to a moonlit olive garden. There, while Jesus was praying, soldiers came, led by Judas—Jesus' own disciple. They arrested Jesus and marched him off to the High Priest, while the disciples ran away in the darkness, all except John and Peter. They crept along behind the soldiers to see what would happen.

At the palace of the High Priest they put Jesus on trial. "Are you the Messiah?" asked the High Priest, with all the gravity of his high office.

"I am," said Jesus calmly.

"Blasphemy," they cried, and they sentenced him to death. They arranged for him to be taken before Pilate, the Roman governor, first thing in the morning; for only Rome could confirm and carry out a death sentence.

Peter and John had crept into the courtyard below. As they led Jesus down from his trial the cock crew, and Peter burst into tears. For now he remembered what Jesus had said at the supper table, and indeed while they had waited, three times he had denied knowing Jesus.

In the dawn light they led Jesus to the great open space in front of Pilate's residence, and demanded that their sentence of death be confirmed and carried out. Pilate questioned Jesus but could not find that he had done anything wrong.

"We have a Law," cried the High Priest, "and by that Law he deserves to die."

Led by agitators, the crowd now started an ugly chant.

"Crucify! Crucify! Crucify him!"

Afraid that there would be a riot, Pilate gave in. He called for a bowl of water, and there at the top of the steps he solemnly washed his hands in sight of all the crowd.

"See," he said, "I am innocent of the blood of this just man. Do with him as you will."

They led Jesus outside the city wall, and there between two thieves on a hill called Calvary, they crucified him.

One of the thieves—perhaps to ease his own pain—jeered at Jesus: "If you are the Son of God, get us down off these crosses." But the other thief rebuked him. "At least we've got what we deserve," he said, "but *he* hasn't done anything wrong." Then turning to Jesus he said, "Master, when you come to your kingdom, remember me."

Jesus replied slowly, for death was very close:

"Indeed I tell you: Today you will be with me—in Paradise."

The sun rose high to noon, and the sky grew dark with menace as if the world would end. At about three in the afternoon Jesus cried with a loud voice: "It is finished." And so he died. But his voice sang with victory, so that the officer in charge of the execution said in awe, "Truly, this was the Son of God."

Easter Morning

Jesus was buried in a garden close by Calvary, in a rock-cut tomb with a great stone rolled across the entrance. Saturday came and went, then early before dawn on Sunday, with the sky grey as a sober suit, Mary Magdalene, one of his friends, came alone from the city. As she came she was weeping, for she had loved Jesus very much. She went into the garden, the dew-drenched grass brushing her ankles in the dark before dawn. She had come to grieve by the tomb of the Lord. But when she came to the tomb she found that the great stone was rolled away from the entrance. She crept up to the dark opening and peered fearfully inside. There, on the shelf, neatly folded, lay the grave-clothes. But Jesus was gone.

Blindly, not knowing what to think, she turned away from the grave. As she did so the sun inched over the horizon, turning to gold the slate-grey roofs of the sleeping city and filling the silent garden with slanting arrows of light.

Under the trees a man was standing. Mary thought he was the gardener.

"Sir," she said. "Sir. If you've taken him—tell me where you've laid him."

"Mary," said the man. But he said it as a man says the name of his beloved, and in that word of two syllables Mary heard the whole truth. "Jesus! Master!" she cried, for it was he. And she fell to her knees. "Do not touch me," he said. "I am not yet ascended to my Father. But go and tell the others that I will meet them in Galilee."

Easter Evening

Later the same day two of Jesus' disciples set out to walk from Jerusalem to the village of Emmaus. As they walked they talked over the events and rumours of the day: Mary's wild story of the man in the garden, and the fact that the tomb was empty.

As they walked they were joined by a stranger.

"Why are you so sad?" he asked.

When they had told him the whole story the stranger smiled.

"You forget," he said, "isn't all this just what the prophets foretold—that the Messiah was bound to suffer like this before coming into his glory?"

So they walked on together, and the stranger explained the Scriptures to them, showing how all the old promises had led to the Messiah, and the Messiah was Jesus. It was like tracing a golden thread in a dark piece of rich cloth.

They came to the village, and the disciples invited the stranger into their cottage. There, by lamplight, the stranger took bread and broke it, as Jesus had done on the night before his death. In that moment they knew. The stranger was Jesus himself. And in the moment of knowing, he vanished out of their sight.

All their tiredness forgotten, the two disciples set off back to Jerusalem through the starlit night.

In an upstairs-room behind locked doors they found the other disciples, and they were greeted with great excitement.

"It's true," they were told. "The Lord has risen. Simon has seen him." "So have we," they answered. And even as they explained, suddenly there was Jesus among them.

"Peace," he said, as they all drew back from him in terror. "It is I. I am not a ghost." And he took food from the table and ate it in front of them.

"I told you," he said, "that the Scriptures must be fulfilled. The Messiah had to die and rise. And now, in my name, the chance of a new start is to be proclaimed to all nations. You are to begin here in Jerusalem and go to all the world. But mark this—I shall send you my Father's promised gift. When you are armed with that power from heaven I shall be with you always, to the world's end."

He took them out on to a hill-side and blessed them, his arms uplifted. In the act of blessing he was parted from them, and none knew the manner of his going.

Fire from Heaven

On the feast day of Pentecost, which was the Jewish feast of harvest, the disciples were all together in a room, talking perhaps of their plans to carry the good news of Jesus to the ends of the world. Suddenly it was as if walls and ceiling had vanished, and a great wind like the wind on a mountain top came roaring around them, filling the house with its sound. It seemed to the disciples as they gazed at one another that each of them was touched by fire, as if they stood with their backs to the sun. It was like seeing what Moses had seen in the burning bush, or what Isaiah had seen in the temple, and somehow they knew that Jesus was present with them. He came in wind and fire, and they were possessed with his Spirit. Like men blown helter-skelter before a hurricane, they lost control. They heard one another babbling strange words in unknown languages.

All this caused quite a turmoil, and before long there was a crowd in the street outside, a gossiping and staring holiday crowd. Some were impressed to hear the foreign languages, but most thought it was all a bit of a joke.

"They've been drinking," someone shouted, and the crowd roared with laughter. But Peter stood up where all could see him, and talked to the crowd.

"Fellow Jews," he shouted. "Listen to me. We're not drunk—after all, it's only nine in the morning . . ." That brought a laugh, and the crowd settled down to listen to this big fisherman.

He reminded them of all God's promises. "This morning," he cried, "you've seen those promises fulfilled." He spoke of Jesus, sent by God, arrested, delivered to the Romans, and killed. He grew in passion as he spoke, until the crowd hung on his words.

"Let all Israel know," he ended, "that God has made this Jesus both Lord and Messiah."

Many of the crowd were deeply moved and asked what they should do.

"Repent," he replied. "Repent and be baptized in the name of Jesus. Your sins will be forgiven, and you will receive the gift of the Holy Spirit."

Stephen

Although there were those who wished to crush it, the new faith spread fast, and one of its most eloquent preachers was a man called Stephen. He was tireless in proclaiming Jesus until there came a day when enemies had him arrested and carried before the High Priest on a charge of blasphemy, like his master before him.

Stephen stood up to speak in his own defence. Starting with Abraham, he rehearsed the whole long history of Israel, showing how the story, from beginning to end, led to Jesus.

"It was Solomon," he cried, "who first built a house of God in this place. But the Most High does not live in houses made by men."

His anger kindled, and he lashed them with a whip of words—as once his master had wielded a leather whip in those sacred precincts.

"You!" he cried. "Heathen at heart, deaf to truth. You always fight against the Holy Spirit. Like father, like son! Was there a prophet your fathers did not persecute? They killed those who foretold the Messiah—you have killed the Messiah himself."

There was a roar of fury in the court, but Stephen was deaf to it.

"Look," he said, gazing up from the dock as if the carved ceiling had opened and he could see into deep heaven. "Look. I can see the Son of Man standing at the right hand of God."

"Blasphemy! Blasphemy!" they screamed. They dragged him from the dock, and out on to the hill-side, where they killed him with stones. As he died, Stephen looked up to heaven.

"Lord Jesus, receive my spirit," he said. He fell to his knees and cried again, "Lord, do not hold this sin against them." So he died. And there was a young man called Saul who watched the murder and approved of all that was done.

Saul

After the death of Stephen, Saul set out on a systematic persecution of the Christian Church. He was a formidable enemy, an educated man, a Rabbi, and a Roman citizen.

He learned that the new faith had been carried to Damascus. So he set out for that city with official papers for the arrest of all who believed in the name of Jesus.

It was noon as they neared Damascus, and the hot, bright sun beat from directly overhead. But to Saul there came a light brighter than the sun, so that he was driven to his knees by its very power. Out of the light there came a voice. "Saul! Why are you persecuting me?" Kneeling there in the road, Saul replied, "Who are you?"

"I am Jesus whom you persecute," said the voice. "But get up. Go into Damascus. I will tell you what you must do."

Saul struggled to his feet, and the light faded. As it faded Saul knew that he was blind.

In the city there was a Christian called Ananias. As he knelt saying his prayers, Jesus spoke to him in a vision:

"Ananias. Go at once to Straight Street. Go to the house of Judas. There you will find a man called Saul. He is blind, and he is expecting a man called Ananias to restore his sight."

"Lord," said Ananias, "I have heard of this man. He has come to Damascus with warrants for our arrest."

But Jesus replied, "I have chosen him to bear witness to me."

So Ananias went. He found Saul, just as the vision had said.

"Saul, my brother," he said, "Jesus has sent me that your sight may be restored, and that you may be filled with the Holy Spirit."

For Saul it was as if scales fell from his eyes, and he could see again. There and then he was baptized by Ananias into the faith of Jesus.

Thereafter Saul devoted all his great talents to spreading the faith of Jesus. And ever afterwards he classed himself among those who had seen Jesus risen from the dead.

Into All the World

In Caesarea there was a Roman centurion called Cornelius. He was a good man and he treated the local Jews well. He had even given them money to build a synagogue.

One day while he was resting in his quarters, Cornelius saw a vision. An angel came to him and said, "Cornelius, your prayers and acts of charity have spoken for you to God. Now this is what you are to do. You must send to Joppa for a man called Simon Peter. He is lodging with another Simon, a tanner, whose house is by the sea-shore."

Next day in Joppa at about noon Simon Peter went up on to the flat roof of the tanner's house to say his prayers while dinner was being prepared. While he was praying he also saw a vision:

Over the sparkling harbour where the fishing-boats tossed, there came down out of the sky an enormous bag made of sailcloth. Peter could see that the bag was full of every kind of animal and bird and insect, numberless and varied as the cargo of Noah's ark. As Peter gazed a voice spoke from heaven: "Peter. It's time for dinner. Slay what you will and eat."

Now of course the Jewish faith, like many ancient religions, laid down strict rules about the sort of food a devout man should eat. Some creatures, like the bullock, were permitted, others, like the pig, were forbidden. Peter replied in horror, "Indeed, Lord, no. I've never eaten anything unclean or against the law."

"What God has made clean, do not you call unclean," cried the voice. This happened three times, and then the vision vanished.

As Peter came back to normal he heard a strange voice speaking his name in the street below. The messengers sent by Cornelius had arrived to take him to Caesarea.

127

When Peter reached Caesarea, the centurion Cornelius met him in the street. The Roman soldier looked at this grizzled fisherman who had come, called by a vision. Slowly, deliberately, he knelt down there in the street as if he recognized in Peter the representative of a power greater even than all the might and majesty of Rome. Peter ran forward and raised the soldier to his feet.

'You must not kneel to me,' he cried. 'I am a man as you are.'

'Together they went into the centurion's quarters, where the soldier had assembled a large gathering of his friends.

Peter spoke to them.

"I hardly need tell you," he said, "that a Jew is forbidden by his religion to have close dealings with a man of another race. But God has shown me quite clearly that I must not call any man unclean. So I have come here without question. And now—what is it that you want of me?"

Then Cornelius explained about his own vision and how he had been commanded to send for Peter. "So," he ended, "we are all met here before God to hear what you have to tell us."

There was a deep silence and they all looked at Peter.

"I now see," he said, "that God has no favourites, but accepts men of all nations who turn to Him." Then he told them of Jesus, of his life and of his death. "But God raised him to life on the third day," he cried, "and allowed him to appear—not to everyone—but to chosen witnesses, to us who ate and drank with him after he rose from the dead. We are to proclaim him to all men, and all who trust him shall receive forgiveness through the power of his name."

As he spoke of the power of the name of Jesus, it was like the day of Pentecost come again. For the Holy Spirit, the Spirit of God, came over them all with the power of wind and fire, and they knew his presence, just as the disciples had known it.

When the turmoil was stilled, Peter cried with great exaltation, "Is anyone prepared to refuse baptism to these Gentiles when they have received the Holy Spirit just as we did ourselves?"

So Cornelius and his household were baptized into the Faith of Jesus, and Christians learned the great truth that the love of God is for all men, whatever the shape of their noses, whatever the colour of their skin.

In the End

The new Faith spread swiftly along the roads of the Roman Empire, under the peace of the disciplined legions, the regiments of the Roman army. But the power of Rome was based on loyalty to the emperor, a loyalty expressed by burning incense before his image as if he were a god. This Christians would not do. They were not disloyal, but there was only one God, and Jesus was His Son—how then could they acknowledge even the emperor as a god? So they were thought to be traitors, and so—as Jesus had warned—they were persecuted.

In one persecution a man called John was imprisoned on the little island of Patmos. There on a Sunday morning, longing to celebrate the Lord's Supper, John had a vision.

Behind him he heard a loud voice like the high sounding of a golden trumpet.

"Write what you see," cried the voice, "and send it to the churches."

He turned to the voice. There stood a figure, like a man, but more—much more—than a man; more real, greater, infinitely more powerful. He wore a long robe with a golden girdle. His hair was white as light, his eyes and his body shone like molten brass in a furnace, his voice was like the thunder of the ocean, and in his right hand he held seven stars.

John knew that he was seeing Jesus, not as the disciples had seen him in human form only, but clothed with all the majesty of God. He fell to the ground as if the vision had killed him.

"Do not be afraid," said the figure, laying a hand on John's head. "I am the first and the last. I am the living one. I was dead but now I am alive for evermore. You are to write down what you have seen, and what you will see."

Then the figure spoke to John about the persecution, and about all who in the long future would suffer for the sake of truth.

"To him who is victorious I will give the right to eat of the Tree of Life that stands in the garden of God. To him who is victorious I will give a white stone, and on it a new name known to none but him that receives it. To him who is victorious I will give the morning star. He shall be robed in white and he shall live for ever in the New Jerusalem which is coming down from God out of heaven."

The vision changed. Now it was as if a door opened in heaven and John looked into the very presence of God. There was a throne; on it a figure gleaming like jasper and cornelian, around it an emerald rainbow. In a circle round the throne were twenty-four men crowned as kings and robed in white. From the throne, with thunder and the flicker of lightning, a voice spoke.

"Holy, holy, holy is God the sovereign Lord of all. He was, and is, and is to come."

The twenty-four kings cried in reply:

"Thou art worthy, O Lord our God, to receive glory and honour and power, because by thy will thou didst create all things."

John looked again. In place of the majestic throne there was a simple lamb. And John remembered how the Baptist had once called Jesus "the Lamb of God". As he remembered, the triumphant shout of the kings changed.

"Worthy is the lamb," they exulted, "the lamb that was slain, to receive power and wealth, wisdom and might, honour and glory and praise."

Again the vision changed. Now it was sombre. There were horses—red, and black, and white, with Death and Destruction riding on them. There were earthquakes, and a moon red as blood, and the stars falling like apples from heaven. There was war and disaster, death and destruction on every side. And John wept bitterly as he saw all that men suffer, all the pain, all the terrible evils that happen in the world God made, and loves, and for which Jesus died.

But the darkness passed like the rolling-up of a picture, and then John saw the final vision.

He saw a new heaven and a new earth, the spring dawn of a new creation. He saw the Holy City—a new Jerusalem—coming down out of heaven. Beautiful she was, like a bride on her wedding-day. So beautiful that John wept again, but now his tears were of joy. Across his weeping a triumphant voice sounded:

"Now at last God has His dwelling among men. He will live with them, and they will be His people. He will wipe away all tears, for there shall be an end of death, and crying and mourning and pain, for the old order has passed away."

Then the figure on the throne—or was it the Lamb?—cried out:

"Behold, I make all things new. I am A and Z, the beginning and the end. To the thirsty I will give water from the well of life."

As the voice cried, John gazed through his tears at the shining city which is the end of all hopes and the fulfilment of all promises. Beautiful beyond all describing, clear as crystal, like a precious jewel. Into that city flooded all the goodness, the skill, the riches, the laughter, courage and nobility of all men from the beginning to the end of time. Now at last all evil and suffering were excluded for ever. Its streets were as gold, its gates as pearls. It needed no light and no place of worship. For God and the Lamb were there, and they are the source of light, and they are the end of worship.

Then John awoke. It was Sunday morning, in prison, on Patmos. Nothing had changed. But John's heart was at peace, for now he knew the meaning of the whole long story and it no longer mattered what happened to him.

So afterwards, when the persecution had spent itself like a burnt-out fire, John wrote his vision in a book. And this is how he ended:

"So be it. Come, Lord Jesus.
The grace of the Lord Jesus be with you all."

He captured the common sense commitment when he categorised animals, the animate, as self-movers. We apply a large range of voluntaristic vocabulary to the behaviour of some animals. They can be frustrated, persistent, unwilling, hesitant, even steadfast and patient.

A test of whether we have really rejected Dualism in our philosophical hearts is whether we are prepared to see agency as a concept that allows of degrees and as a reality which has evolved from the appetitive life of the animal kingdom. A benefit of concentrating on expressive behaviour is that it serves to undermine the glib dualist contrast between active, wilful behaviour and passive will-less bodily events. Too often we think of human actions as the outcome of deliberate processes of cognition and calculation issuing finally in a moment of decision, in which we move our bodies to act. When we are sceptical about the presence of such high level cognitive capacities in animals we are tempted to conclude that everything which an animal body does is a matter of something happening to it.

Expression, however, though it is action, is not easily describable as either active or passive. Someone tells a joke and we laugh. We can be helpless with laughter or we can laugh out of a sense of social politeness. We are sensitive, perhaps hyper-sensitive to the embarrassed laugh, the forced laugh, the nervous laugh. Laughter allows of a whole range of degrees of control, helplessness, spontaneity and contrivance. But in most cases we are at a loss to say whether our response is involuntary or chosen. The distinction between spontaneous and forced, which does apply to expressions, runs parallel to the active/passive distinction, but is very different. It refers to the pressures and compulsions of social interactions which are different from the causes and outcomes of physical processes. Laughing because the joke is funny is not describable in terms of a stark contrast between autonomous action and determined behaviour.

Still, one way in which it becomes clear that expressions are actions of agents is that they can be modulated. We teach children to control their expressions of frustration or anger and even of distress. This training involves a moulding of their inner lives; it is not merely an attempt to keep the peace in the playground or supermarket. There is a close connection between the nature and intensity of feelings and the way we express them. Cries can be loud

be natural to look to the animal sciences.

But, according to a dominant strand of thought in the animal sciences, there is no gap to close. We do not stand to non-human animals as the aliens stand to us. When we do not include animal minds in our stock-taking of the sentient world, nothing real has been left out. One task of the animal sciences is to remind us that we are not mistaken in our stock-taking. Despite the powerful temptations to think otherwise, no one is waving, to us or to anything else.

The point of the story of the alien is to identify just what part of the world it is that they miss if they do not recognise the reality of our point of view. They fail to see us waving. But it also identifies the kind of thing *we* are missing when we deny that other animals could have points of view. The pieces of world that we miss, or misdescribe, are those objects and events which, as a matter of fact, make up a creature's *expressive behaviour*.

If we are really to get to grips with the problem of animal minds then we must understand the key role of expression, not only in recognising other minds, but in the very idea of another mind. It is therefore to the structures of the expressive life that we now turn.

expression in general

There is a difference between telling somebody about something and expressing something to somebody. This is not a merely semantic point: 'Expression' is a portmanteau word, it can refer to any type of utterance, any sort of speaking out, including 'expressions' of opinion. But it has a more specific sense. We talk of 'expressions of feeling', or of 'expressing oneself'. In these senses there is a suggestion of disclosure, of revealing something about oneself or of sharing one's experience. It implies a directness of communication between one person and another which is not involved in descriptions or reports even of one's subjective experience. There is much more going on in such transactions than we might think if our only model of personal communication is the storing and transmission of information.

There is a complex structure even to the most everyday exchanges, whenever people laugh together, insult each other, invite each other for a drink, when one person acknowledges another person in any way. Typical examples of expression in this sense of direct personal communication would be: Norm spoke irritably to

Norma; Norm is sulking because he did not get his own way; Norm and Norma clung on to each other in fear.

The shape of this structure can be detected by putting a series of questions to an instance of expression: who, with what, expressed what, about what, to whom and in what context? These six questions (see below) bring out relevant features of expression:

A Who?	Norm	**Agent**
B With what?	Voice	**Medium**
C What?	Nostalgia	**Content**
D About what?	Tyneside	**Intentional object**
E To whom?	Norma	**Receptor**
F In what context?	In the bar at the Free Trade Inn	**Context**

The above represents the situation in which Norm expresses to Norma his nostalgia for Tyneside by singing *The Blaydon Races* in the bar at the Free Trade Inn. These elements fall into four groups which are features of expression in general.

- A implies *agency*.
- B implies *embodiment*.
- C and D imply *determinacy of sense*.
- E and F imply a *community of expression*.

What we want to suggest is that whether animals have *minds* can be understood as a set of questions about whether the lives of animals exhibit these characteristics of expression. And the further question, *can we understand* anything about animal minds depends on whether we can position ourselves in such a way that these features of expression become visible to us. In what follows, we shall try to make these ideas more precise.

expression and agency

Expression is a type of action. We attribute many aesthetic qualities to natural sounds and movements but there are numerous qualities that apply only to expressive behaviour because they imply agency: repressed, unrestrained, uncertain, tentative, bombastic, forced, spontaneous, hysterical, controlled.

This immediately raises a fundamental problem. To take seriously the expressions of animals and our interactions with them is to attribute agency to animals; and if agency, the nightmare continues, freedom; and if freedom, the end of the determinist model of animal behaviour without which it cannot be susceptible to scientific investigation. This is close to the heart of the opposition to participative methodologies in animal studies and of the advocacy of an exclusively objective approach. The attribution of agency to non-humans must be the worst extravagance of anthropomorphic thinking and the end of scientific understanding.

Agency is seen as an obstacle to scientific understanding because it is thought of as outside the natural order. For this reason, the rejection of non-objective methodologies is often inspired by a clandestine Dualism of determined system and 'free will'. If the clandestine dualist, like the overt dualist of the past, wishes to separate human beings from the natural order, he may welcome the idea that human agency is exempt from scientific scrutiny. If, however, he looks forward to the day when human behaviour will be scientifically explicable like any other natural phenomena, he may merely tolerate the human exemption on a temporary basis. But in either case there can be no exemption for brute animals who are already fully paid up members of the natural order. For the clandestine dualist, we cannot allow agency to animals without applying to them full citizenship and the moral standing of a Kantian autonomous agent. We ought to hang wolves for sheep-stealing and we ought never to use them as means to an end, human or otherwise.

Our intuitive attitude to animals, on the other hand, assumes that there is no dichotomy between human agency and animal behaviour. We do not make a single absolute distinction between the dynamisms of animal life and the 'will' we attribute to ourselves. As Aristotle[2] pointed out, we apply the distinction between voluntary and involuntary to animal action as well as to human action.

or soft. The human infant has a range of chortles and gurgles and a repertoire of cries from whimpers to full-blown screams. New research is constantly revealing how sophisticated this early human behaviour is. Even the volume of the cry is not just a matter of decibels. Cries are repressed or hysterical; they manifest anything from hyper-control to loss of control. So, too, an animal which can express its feelings can modulate that expression.

The possibility of modulation is important. Expression acquires its communicative content through being at one point rather than another in a range of possible modulations. In this way, a particular expression acquires a role in a communicative exchange. This is not true of those manifestations of feelings which are not expressions. Some people blush more than others. And the same person may blush more deeply on one occasion than on another. The depth of the blush is perhaps an *indication*, evidence, of the depth of the embarrassment. But we cannot use the gradation of blush as a means of communicating how embarrassed we are.

The expressive repertoire of any creature, including humans, is rooted in its species nature. Expression is always tied to physiology. Display preening is a possible mode of expression only for creatures with bills. A complex muscular structure is necessary for facial expression. The mating rituals of cats, the territorial disputes of Thompson's gazelles, the colour changes of octopuses, are natural to members of those species. They are constitutive of the ways these animals go about their business and earn their living. It was such modes of animal expression that fascinated Darwin.[3]

These patterns of expressive behaviour can be triggered in inappropriate circumstances. This suggests to some that they occur at all only because of their functional significance as adaptive behaviour. But it does not follow from the idea that expressive behaviour is the product of evolutionary inputs that it has no significance for the animal whose behaviour it is. There may be an ingenious explanation of the functional significance of laughter but, when we laugh, we do not feel ourselves to be, and we are not victims of alien forces from the past. There is a danger that this is the way we think of animals when we describe what they do as *merely* 'instinctive', 'automatic', or 'mechanistic'. As we have seen, an important assumption amongst some animal scientists is that to say behaviour is 'instinctive' is to deny that the creature has desires and carries out intentions. And in the absence of such cognitive activity there can be nothing which it is like for the creature to do these things. This involves a false contrast between, on the one hand, the bodily, the passive and the natural, and on the other, the cognitive, active and conventional. Expressions are the actions that come naturally, yet they are still actions. An animal's expressive behaviour is bodily but that does not mean that its behaviour is something its body does to it.

So the fact that an animal's expressive behaviour is biologically determined does not mean that it is not really expressive. But equally at the other end of the scale of sophistication, the fact that expressive behaviour can become highly conventionalised does not mean that it is not really bodily. Humans, and other creatures, can come to gain high degrees of control over the expressive repertoires available to them. The courtiers at Versailles evolved elaborate rituals to express deference and disdain: genuine expression despite its artificiality. The English say 'Ouch', the French 'Aiee', but both conventionalised expressions can be involuntary exclamations. The sardonic smile is a relatively simple contortion of the face which nevertheless requires an enormously complex social context if it is to succeed as a communication.

What this suggests is that the conventions that constitute language arise not from rules devised to map reality in a mental medium, but from the ever-increasing modulation of expressive interactions. If we want to regard language-use as part of, and not in opposition to, the natural order, we should try to see language, fundamentally, not as a species of representation, but as a kind of ultra-modulated expression. It also suggests that if we really want to abandon Dualism, both overt and clandestine, we should employ the concept of expression as a means of undermining the absolute contrast between cognitive activity and bodily passivity.

expression and embodiment

Expression is not only something we do, we do it in and through our bodies. If we recognise expression for what it is, we recognise it as the action of an *embodied agent*. This may seem obvious. How else could we express our thoughts and feelings except through our bodily actions?

However, the resistance to involving agency in physical reality runs deep. On some accounts of what the world is, there is no room for physical agency. For example, some types of determinists are so unfriendly to the notion of agency that they would prefer to deny its possibility rather than accommodate it in a world of cause and effect.

Again, on some accounts of what we are, bodies *cannot* be expressive. The dualist account is just such a story. As we saw earlier, if one ambition of Descartes' theory was to render the mind unworldly, another was to make the dualist body 'unmindly'. The dualist makes the body secure for science by overcoming our natural disposition to treat bodies as bearers of meaningful communication. All psychological elements had to be transferred over to mind. This transference allows the dualist body to be defined by the methodologies of the physical sciences.

As a result, the human body is rendered incapable of carrying communicative significance. And so, since meaning is not carried by the outer states of the body, it must be carried by the inner states of the mind. Since the body cannot speak, it must be that we speak out of it.

So, the dualist body, de-souled, is not capable of expression. What it manifests are not psychological states but tantalising if inconclusive *evidence* about the mind and meanings hidden within. The dualist body is a mass not of expression but of symptoms. Their relation to the psychological states beneath is contingent, external, evidential. Whereas the relation of expression to the states expressed is conceptual, internal, constitutive.

Hence, to say expression is the action of an *embodied* agent has a point. If we want to avoid reducing expression to mere movement, we cannot give a dualist account of the body. This means that a dualist account of the disembodied mind and an account which recognises the role of expression are incompatible.

When people used to think seriously about disembodied minds, in the form of angels, they realised that the only form of communication possible between them was some form of 'pre-established harmony'. That is, precisely because they lacked bodies, angels could not communicate their thoughts to each other. Rather, God so arranged matters that each angel had the appropriate beliefs about the experiences of its fellows in sequence, in such a way that it mimicked genuine communication. Such intellectual ingenuity strikes us as amusing today, but medieval thinkers[4] at least grasped that there was a real problem about the idea of disembodied creatures communicating.

This is an insight which seems to have escaped more contemporary speculation about disembodied communication. The fantasy of telepathy is fuelled by disappointment with normal means of communication. In popular mythology, telepathy is regarded as noise-free, frictionless communion of minds – as an ideal form of communication. But even if telepathy were real, it could not deliver communication. What it delivers is a happy *consonance* of thought – you think of the Ace of Spades and, perhaps after some negligible delay, I think of the same card. But in this case there is no difference between my receiving the thought 'The card is the Ace of Spades' and my simply having the thought 'The card is the Ace of Spades'. There is nothing to indicate that this thought has been *communicated* to me by someone else. Even if my thought matches the value of hidden cards more often than chance would predict, what we have to explain is not miraculous communication but miraculous guesswork. It is for this reason that telepathy is not the expression of thought but the transportation of thoughts from one mind to another.

Perhaps it is envisaged that telepathically communicated thoughts are recognisable as communicated because they come in the 'voice' of the sender. In my mind, I 'hear' you 'say' 'It's the Ace of Spades!' In this case telepathy *is* construed as a form of communication. But the ideal of mentally hearing someone's voice is clearly parasitic upon the idea of hearing someone's voice in the normal way. And in this case, telepathy is not an ideal form of communication because it escapes the contingencies of normal expression but, on the contrary, is subject to the same constraints, except this time in a preternatural form. We shall have exchanged a happy consonance for an unhappy medium.

It takes an effort not to see a body as bearing meaning. In the human case we have to go to great lengths to fail to see the human body as significant. We read bodies constantly. Of course we are on the look-out for particular displays of emotion, the angry gesture, the slumped form of depression, the smile of recognition. But our sensitivity to others is more general than that. We are aware of the presence of others and the character of that presence. Attending to the deportment of people crossing the street, we can see the difference between the meandering walk of the sight-seer and the purposeful walk of the person going about their business. Our social competence, and indeed survival, depends on the capacity to tell the difference between the clenched fist and the open palm and all the variations in between.

Body-language has been a topic of great interest to anthropologists and psychologists. Although the motives that underlie its popularity may be prurient, there are advantages in having a 'language' which is an unlearnt (and therefore universal) and a largely uncontrolled (and therefore reliable) medium of communication of feeling. It would provide a route through what people actually express to what they really mean and feel. But even if body language could satisfy the Peeping Toms of the soul, its philosophical significance is less impressive. If we accept that the Other Minds Problem is a genuine problem, the supposed universality and reliability of body language will not solve it for us. If there is no bridge between what happens on the surface of our bodies and what happens in our minds then the fact, if it is a fact, that certain surface behaviour is universal will make no difference. Nor can the supposed reliability of body language constitute the communicative content of behaviour. All it means is that we have reason to trust it more than explicit communication. What body language means is unexplained by the fact, if it is a fact, that we can trust what it says.

Nevertheless body language reminds us of the extent to which we live in an environment of meaning. We are surrounded by the living and breathing embodiments of thought, desire and intention. It takes a great deal of effort to lose this sense, to become body-blind. But people have made the effort. Descartes requires us to break down the environment of meaning into the thinking self and matter in motion. It became a mark of philosophical sophistication that one could seriously (in the way philosophers are serious) entertain the possibility of solipsism.

There is perhaps little damage done by the extravagant thought experiments of philosophers. But there are more sinister practical programmes of de-signification, which bring a moral dimension to these issues. Where large-scale acts of inhumanity take place it seems necessary first to reduce the victims to a state of physical wretchedness to make possible the discounting of their human, personal or spiritual status. The routines of concentration camps were designed to make the inmates and their feelings invisible to their oppressors.

Critics of animal experimentation draw analogies between our treatment of animals and these large-scale notorious acts of cruelty and oppression. They believe that the denial or discounting of animal experience runs parallel to man's inhumanity to man. They accuse the scientific enterprise of inducing and reinforcing insensitivity to animal suffering through the advocacy of inappropriate methodologies. Behaviourism is a methodology to secure body-blindness.

Many think that the views and campaigns of the animal rights activists are extravagant. Still, they are likely to be just as alarmed when those who conduct animal research, like Kennedy, not only deny that any animals are conscious but readily acknowledge that common sense, or as he sees it, our genetic programming, says otherwise. Far from this making him re-think his position, he recommends various techniques for suspending our intuitive judgements and their moral implications in order to stiffen our methodological backbones.

How is body-blindness possible? Expression is invisible outside of communicative relationships. Recognising expression, like understanding meaning, is not a matter of speculation but of insider-dealing. It involves the opposite of the sort of objectivity which requires distance, detachment and the abandonment of personal perspectives. Body-blindness is sometimes self-induced because scientific methodology seems to demand it.

In the animal sciences, where we find traces of residual Dualism about meaning and mind, we find a downplaying of the role of bodily expression. Conversely, insisting on the expressive values of embodiment, whether human or animal, should fortify us against the tendency to do 20th-century science with 16th-century theories of mind.

expression and determinacy of sense

We saw earlier that there is a real problem about specifying the content of animal beliefs. We want to say that the animal's behaviour must have intentional significance but we are at a loss to say what this significance is without lapsing into what seems to be anthropomorphism. We saw that there was a need to reduce the tension between our belief that animal behaviour does often have intentional significance and the requirement that intentional significance exhibits sufficient 'determinacy of sense'. We saw that we could do something to reduce this tension by recognising that the determinacy of our own thought and talk is not something fixed objectively, independently of human ways of going on. We now need to connect this idea with the role that expression plays in the lives of non-language using animals.

It might first be thought that the problems that arose about the content of animal beliefs also arise about animal expressions. Some expressions are expressions of mental states that have definite cognitive content. If I whimper at the approach of the lion, an adequate account of my behaviour will have to include my beliefs that this is a lion, that lions are dangerous, that I am in jeopardy, etc. Similarly, if the lion snarls at me, an adequate account of its behaviour will have to include its belief about what I am for it. An intruder, a rival or a meal.

The logic of this argument is that because we cannot recognise a piece of behaviour as expressive unless we can say of what it is the expression, and because we cannot do that until we can imagine what representations fill the mental space of the animal mind, we cannot attribute subjective experience to it. So until we can, for example, determine how the mouse represents the cat to itself, we cannot say it is frightened of it. Representation precedes communication could be the slogan for this view and, if it is true, appealing to expression will not help us to understand animal minds.

From this perspective, what makes a piece of behaviour expressive is that the component bodily movements happen to be connected with internal states with a particular content. But if this were true we could imagine a creature that is only ever in one particular state, and this state always and only triggers one type of expressive behaviour. We could imagine a dog which could only emit a particular and invariant bark. If we apply this conception to the real world and to real dogs, it will be tempting to think that the significance of some particular piece of barking can also be determined in isolation from the rest of its behaviour.

But, as we have seen, putting things this way round inevitably generates scepticism about the determinacy of the psychological states which are doing the work. All the weight determining the significance of behaviour is placed on the determinate nature of psychological states. But what is supposed to give these states their determinate nature? In our own case the issue of determinacy of sense is raised and resolved in linguistic terms: what do you mean by 'such and such'? I mean 'so and so'. Indeed it is hard to address a sensible question about determinacy of sense to a non-linguistic animal. Such questions imply a search, which has no place in the life of non-language-users for greater precision or a removal of ambiguity. We know and the dog knows where the scared cat went, but where do we put the scare quotes in the sentence 'What is the dog believing when it believes the cat is up the tree?'?

This combination of thoughts, that psychological states must carry the content and that there is no medium to enable this, fuels scepticism about our knowledge of animal minds.

At this point we can either try to live with the metaphysical mysteriousness of the medium of thought or we can try to answer the question. One answer is unsatisfactory but attractive to contemporary thinkers. The content of psychological states is determined by the representational character of the neural states with which they are identical. The lion can notice the antelope by the pool because its brain can be in a state which represents that antelope by that pool. It is the capacity of the lion's nervous system to be in determinate states which ultimately allows us to say that the lion's behaviour has some determinate significance.

The trouble is that, at present, we have little idea how such neural states come to determine psychological states. So, in general, the legitimacy of our ordinary talk about animals' thoughts and feelings depends upon a theoretical solution to the mind/brain problem along empiricist lines. And the correctness of any particular ascription will remain unknown until we are in a position to use such a theory to make particular predictions. In the absence of the theory, the only tenable position is scepticism. For proponents of this view, the prognosis for our understanding of animal minds is present failure relieved by hope of future success.

But, if Wittgenstein was right, and communication precedes the possibility of representation, then the whole idea of neural representations which objectively fix the content of psychological states is a mistake. Objects and structures, including brains, can represent other objects and structures only if they are taken to be representations by conscious beings. The concept of representation is supposed to explain how it is that thought and talk can be about anything. But if representations are not free-standing, they do not explain but require that thought and talk can be about something. The capacity to represent something is not some fundamental property of parts of the physical world. Viewed objectively, no part of the world can represent anything at all. Rather, representation is a kind of activity in which some animals can engage.

The priority of communication over representation requires and allows us to think differently about the determinacy of psychological states. What is plainly wrong is to demand of a non-linguistic animal determinacy of sense that applies only to the experience of language-using animals. We cannot model the required determinacy of the psychological states of non-language-using creatures on the linguistic determinacy exhibited by language-using creatures. And it would compound the error if, having failed to elicit a response to the demand for linguistic determinacy, one were to conclude that, as it were, some vagueness infects the animal's life, that its experience is always slightly out of focus.

Instead we can seek to use the concept of expression to sharpen the focus of the animal's psychological states. Determinacy of psychological states is secured not by the articulate structure of the medium in which representations occur. It is secured by expressive behaviour. The content of the psychological state of an animal is fixed by the place of the characteristic expression of that state in the repertoire of expressive behaviour available to the animal.

expression and community

Expressions are other-directed. Though we can smile to ourselves or, like Susan Nipper in *Dombey & Son*, at no one in particular, we do not produce a smile and then decide to cast it in someone's direction. No more can one produce an arrow which does not point. The directedness of a smile is not a matter of inference. For example, you return the smile of an attractive stranger who was in fact smiling at another. Though errors may have led you into the predicament, your acknowledgement is not a mistaken inference but a form of social bungling. Recognising a smile involves recognising a directed expression; realising that the smile is directed at oneself is to experience oneself caught up in a significant relationship. This does not mean that expressions are experienceable only from the first person point of view. John smiles at Mary. It is not only John who is aware of the smile. Mary and Mary's mother may well be too. Second and third person perspectives are just as good as first. We can be aware of our own expressions, of being the recipient of the expressions of others or the observer of the expressive exchanges of others. In all cases we are required to be in the personal mode. The third person point of view is still a personal point of view. It is to be distinguished from the push towards an objective standpoint which aims at maximum abstraction from the perspectival.

Expression can only be understood from an insider's perspective because it is a social reality. It characterises social animals; it develops within social relationships; it is reinforced by social recognition (infants who are not smiled at stop smiling) and can be distorted or destroyed by social pathologies.

Some philosophers have attacked what they call 'folk psychology'. They have argued that our ordinary psychological concepts contain a pre-scientific understanding of our mental states; as scientific knowledge advances, they suggest, we come to realise that our familiar psychological concepts are radically distorted and embody a false view of what we call the 'mind'. If this claim is established then psychological concepts do not even apply to us, let alone to non-human animals.

But psychological language is expressive, not representational. Psychological concepts (I think, she intends, we feel, etc.) get their primary sense from their role in exchanges between paid-up members of the human communication society, not by their theoretical power or plausibility. Using them, we share our feelings, influence each other and exchange information. Folk psychology is not a reconstruction of our inner lives, so it is not a false reconstruction.

Our psychological concepts do not embody a theory of the human mind. Therefore, their application to the non-human cannot take the form of the extension of a scientific theory from one domain to another. We may, for example, construct neurological theories about the nervous system of one species and then determine empirically to what extent they apply to another. But if we apply the concepts of folk psychology to non-human animals the extension cannot take the same form.

Whether we can apply these concepts to non-human animals is not a matter of justifying the extension of a theory beyond the human case but of recognising the viability of certain relationships. This explains why there will always be a moral dimension to discussions about animal minds. Matters of recognition are always matters of acknowledgement as well as knowledge, of discretion as well as objective judgement. In other words, they are always about our commitments as well as our capacity to understand our environment. The issue is what sorts of relationships across the species barrier we are prepared to recognise and enter into. Not only what do we know, but what company do we want to keep? And on what terms?

If this is right, the problem of understanding other animal minds is not, in the end, an epistemic knowledge problem at all. If we think of personal communication in terms of the contemporary concept of information transfer we need never refer to people or the subjective view at all. It is not because expressive behaviour is objectively visible that I am entitled to conclude that you are sending messages to me. This epistemological order needs to be reversed. It is because I am receiving messages from you (i.e. the creature belongs to a community of possible recipients) that your expressive behaviour is visible at all.

The Problem of Other Minds can be seen as a misguided way of pointing this out. What the problem demonstrates is not that we cannot know each other. It shows us that our relations with one another are not, at bottom, founded on knowledge at all. We have to have the right kind of relation to one another, before we can begin to speak of knowledge. Similarly, thinking of animals as automata treats the limits of our ability to relate to animals as a deficiency in knowledge. This deficiency becomes enshrined in false theories and impoverished methodologies. But, in reality, the scepticism about the minds of animals that is endemic in the animal sciences is neither prudent modesty about what we can know, nor just a kind of mistake about what, in fact, we do know. It is a failure at the level of primary communication.

What this means is not that we fail to understand animals because we do not have access to their experiences. This way of putting the matter both understates and over-generalises the difficulty. The difficulty is that we do not feature in the lives of most animals. Hence we are never or only rarely the object of their expressive attention. For us there is no communication without recognising each other as creatures who have a view on the world, who respond to it and act in it and upon it, and who express themselves out of that experience. Our expressive community is formed by those who acknowledge others from the base of their own experience, recognising the others' right to voice their view of the world and their unique entitlement to express their reactions to it.

The real problem of other animal minds is a challenge to us to expand this expressive community; to find ways of interacting with our neighbour species, extending our capacity to recognise other creatures in their expressive presence in the world.

This does not involve treating non-human animals as autonomous Kantian persons. We do not treat most people most of the time as if they were. Not the young, nor the old, the mentally ill, the bereaved, the emotionally upset, the nervous, the startled, the drunk nor the depressed. It is only in ghettos of society, artificially maintained for specific purposes, such as law courts and boardrooms, that strict autonomy is enforced. We are quite used to unequal relationships in the expressive community. All of us begin life by being inducted into it long before we are capable of being fully competent members. We acquire competence through the co-operative acknowledgement of others who initiate and sustain relationships into which we grow. So the need to extend the range and depth of our relationships with animals is not undermined by the fact that this will not be a partnership of equals. It can still be possible to find methodologies which both extend our relationships with other animals and which also provide genuinely scientific data.

conclusion

If we restrict our account of the lives of other animals to the vocabulary of physics, then no amount of evidence could be sufficient to justify the conclusion that we share our world with other minds and kinds of mind. This is not because the evidence is unavailable or uncertain or insufficient. It is because the very idea of evidence for minds in this sense has been both required and ruled out by definition.

The idea of expression is fundamental here not because it is a kind of super-evidence, one that can find a place in the vocabulary of physics despite the odds against it. Reading behaviour as expressive is not attending to a kind of evidence at all. What the idea does is to remind us that the vocabulary of physics is not the only, and not even the most useful way, of getting at all there really is in the world. The reality of some things in the world is only available, not through abstracting from our human lives as embodied creatures who interact with others, but by attending to our interactions more carefully. Amongst those things are animal minds.

Of course, if we have doubts about whether animals have minds at all, it is no good appealing to the fact of expressive behaviour. For to have these doubts is, amongst other things, not to see the